Computer Consulting on Your Home-Based PC

Other books in the Entrepreneurial PC Series

Health Service Businesses on Your Home-Based PC, *Rick Benzel*

Bookkeeping on Your Home-Based PC, *Linda Stern*

Mailing List Services on Your Home-Based PC, *Linda Rohrbaugh*

The Entrepreneurial PC: The Complete guide to Starting a PC-Based Business —2nd Edition, *Bernard J. David*

Computer Consulting on Your Home-Based PC

Herman Holtz

Windcrest®/McGraw-Hill

New York San Francisco Washington, D.C. Auckland Bogotá Caracas
Lisbon London Madrid Mexico City Milan Montreal New Delhi
San Juan Singapore Sydney Tokyo Toronto

pbk   3 4 5 6 7 8 9 10 11 FGR/FGR 9 9 8 7 6 5
hc   2 3 4 5 6 7 8 9 10 11 FGR/FGR 9 9 8 7 6 5 4

Library of Congress Cataloging-in-Publication Data

Holtz, Herman.
    Computer consulting on your home-based PC / by Herman Holtz.
        p.   cm.
    Includes index.
    ISBN 0-8306-4448-2   ISBN 0-8306-4490-0 (pbk.)
    1. Business consultants.   2. Electronic data processing
consultants.   I. Title.
HD69.C6H6198   1993
001'.0285'416—dc20
                                                                93-10119
                                                                CIP

Acquisitions editor: Brad Schepp
Editorial team: Margaret Myers, Editor
                Joanne Slike, Executive Editor
Production team: Katherine G. Brown, Director
                Susan E. Hansford, Coding
                Patsy D. Harne, Layout
                Joan Wieland, Proofreading
Design team: Jaclyn J. Boone, Designer   EPC1
                Brian Allison, Associate Designer   4424
Cover design by Lori E. Schlosser
Marble paper background courtesy of Douglas M. Parks, Blue Ridge Summit, Pa.

Contents

Foreword
Advice for a
new PC consultant

Schools in the old days emphasized the "three Rs"—reading, writing, and 'rithmetic. I believe that in home-based PC consulting there are also three fundamental "Rs"—reputation, results, and referrals. Everything a consultant does should contribute to at least of one of those three Rs.

Reputation is a combination of your business ethics and the general perception of your skills by the client community. Your reputation is one of your most valuable assets; protect it at all costs.

Reputation

The best way to protect your reputation is treat your clients fairly. Avoid projects for which you lack the qualifications unless the client is fully aware of that lack and still wishes to proceed. Don't gossip about clients or reveal proprietary information. Tell your clients about any relationships that might lead to a financial gain outside normal consulting fees. For example, if you have chosen to include product sales to supplement your consulting, let clients know about it up front.

License any software that you use. If it's commercial, buy a copy. If you use shareware, be sure to send in the suggested registration fee.

Join a user group, ideally related to your specialty. For example, if you specialize in Novell networks, join a Novell users group. If none is available locally for your specialty, join the user group focused on the specialty nearest to it, or help start a new user group for your specialty area. Local product vendors can often give you contact information for user groups.

Once you're a member, be helpful. Contribute to the newsletter, give a presentation at a meeting, share a trick you've learned, answer questions posed by other members of the group. After all, you are positioning yourself as an expert on this area, so what better place to showcase your knowledge, meet people interested in this topic, and help others at the same time? Don't try to sell your services directly at a meeting or be arrogant about your knowledge. If a question comes up that no one can answer, consider researching a solution once you are back in your office.

What you do next depends on the level of effort involved, and your current marketing strength. If the answer is relatively easy to determine and it's unlikely that you can translate it into consulting services, write it up for the newsletter. However, the primary purpose of all this is to generate paying clients, so know when to stop giving away information.

Consider joining a trade or professional association. Trade associations typically have businesses as members and promote that industry. Professional associations have individuals as members and deliver services to develop and improve the person. Through an association, you have the opportunity for continuing education in business and professional development. Also, if you carefully select your association, you will be mingling with potential clients. They'll get to know you better, and might call you when they need someone with your specialty.

If your marketing niche is small business, consider the local Chamber of Commerce. In addition, there are vendor-specific organizations such as the Apple Programmers and Developers Association, or the Microsoft Developers Network. A list of over a hundred such associations may be found in *The Computer Industry Almanac* (Brady), an annual publication by Karen and Egil Juliussen.

Another way to gain visibility as an expert is to participate in electronic bulletin boards or commercial online services such as CompuServe. Locate the message areas for your specialty, learn the general forum rules, and then begin making your contribution. When you start seeing your name in statements from others such as, "That's a tough question, why not ask. . . ," it's a good sign that you have established a technical image.

Results

Clients are most interested in what you can do for them. Rather than dazzling them with your technical expertise, think about their needs. As Nido Qubein often mentions in his speeches, "Find out what keeps them awake at night, and then solve their most pressing problem." To do this well, you have to stand back from technology and try to get a broader business view of a project. Understanding the problem greatly increases your chances for success. Nobody cares about an elegant solution that doesn't address the client's primary needs.

Referrals

A referral is the most powerful way to get clients. However, people first need to know about the services you provide, and then think of you when an opportunity happens. Be sure that people know where and how to reach you, as well as what you do. As the Iowa-area contact for the Independent Computer Consultants Association, I am amazed at how often I meet consultants seeking new business who lack such basic marketing tools as a business card. I find it even stranger when I get a business card that lacks a mailing address or a telephone number. PC consulting is a competitive field; don't make clients play guessing games.

Make sure that not only potential clients, but also those who might advise them, know your specialty and how to reach you. For example, if you provide training, make sure that computer retail outlets know about your business. If you design and install LAN cabling, get to know building contractors and facilities managers. My newsletter mailing list includes accountants, bankers, and lawyers who are regularly advising companies that could be future clients.

Plan, plan, plan. Plan your cash flow. Plan your marketing. Plan your business strategies. Accept that you don't know all the answers; most of the rest of us don't either. Planning is not a process that you do once and forget. Review and revise your plans at least once a year when you are well-established, more often if you're just getting started.

The power of planning

—*Dorothy A. Creswell, CAM, CDP*

(Mrs. Creswell is president of her own independent computer consulting firm, D C Consulting, Inc., of Ankeny, Iowa. She also manages to find time in her busy schedule to be active in the Independent Computer Consultants Association at both the national and local levels.)

Introduction
The PC & the consultant

This book is written for the independent home-based PC consultant—a most modern profession, one that has existed for only about a decade. However, the background of the computer-support industry in general, in the days before the appearance of the PC, is relevant to understanding the role of the independent home computer consultant of today. Much of what today's PC consultant does is similar to the more traditional work of computer consulting as practiced in connection with mainframe computers, although there are also some important differences.

One important difference is the size of the consultant's typical client. Today, the smallest organizations, even one-person ventures, own desktop computers as fully capable as the mainframes of a few years ago. Many of today's computer owners need help in coping with computer needs, as did the owners of the earlier digital behemoths. The number of clients for computer consulting services has thus exploded, along with the soaring proliferation of computers.

Another difference is that of software availability. Only a few years ago, the computer consultant was typically someone who supported operation and maintenance of the mainframe computers, often on-site as a temporary employee of the client or of a consulting company serving the client. Computer consultants have always provided many sophisticated services necessary in the computer milieu, primarily in the software area. There were relatively few independent computer consultants in the beginning, except for those who worked as technical temporaries and called themselves independent computer consultants.

Computer owners needed such experts to design their systems, specify hardware and software, write programs, solve software and hardware problems, keep the systems up to date, and even operate the systems. For the most part, there was little off-the-shelf software, and owners could use little of what was available without extensive modification. A large part of the computer consultant's activity consisted of creating custom software for computer owners, and revising existing programs to run more efficiently or provide additional features. In many cases, long-term contracts were let to revise and improve existing programs and otherwise support the organization's computer facilities and systems. The Postal Service, for example, let a contract to revise their main payroll program for greater

Computer consulting history

efficiency because it required 24 hours to run. In fact, many computer consultants report that the bulk of their work is repairing existing programs that need improvements of various kinds to solve problems, improve their efficiency, and add features, which in many cases should have been in the original version. Much of this work is carried out under the euphemism of "software maintenance."

Many computer owners have their own in-house computer specialists, but prefer or are compelled by circumstance to reinforce their in-house capabilities by calling on consultant experts for many of the necessary peripheral tasks. These can include analyzing clients' problems and identifying their needs, writing new programs or modifying and adapting existing programs to the client's requirements, designing data-collection systems and data-entry forms, carrying out data-entry operations, and even functioning as full-time computer operators and actually running the large and costly systems. (Many of the government's computer installations are run by contractors, for example.) Despite the many new developments and changes in computers and the ways in which they are used, the main trend of the work done by consultants continues to be the design, development, and maintenance of software systems and programs.

A great change in computer consulting came about with the development of the PC. Unfortunately, for those large corporations already entrenched in manufacturing and selling mainframe computers, they did not at first comprehend what was happening. They did not take the PC seriously because they did not understand the dynamic nature of the technology. Even more unfortunate and inexplicable, they lacked the vision to understand the many unfilled needs this revolutionary new asset would satisfy, the applications to which it would be put. They regarded this new breakthrough as a gadget, as little more than a toy or, at best, something to amuse hobbyists.

That myopia might have been due, in part at least, to the nature of the new computer experts versus the entrenched old guard: The interlopers were, almost without exception, bright youngsters of the day. Many were teenagers, in fact, with completely open minds and great imagination. The "old men" of the computer establishment probably found it difficult to take brilliant teenagers seriously as the pioneers of an important and revolutionary new direction computers were about to take.

That attitude changed—it could not do otherwise—as PCs began appearing on millions of desks in homes and offices everywhere, with capabilities rapidly approaching and even exceeding those of mainframe computers and vast libraries of commercial software programs readily available for use directly off the shelf.

Computer consulting today

A significant change has come about in computer consulting: There is a new breed of computer consultant, serving many needs that did not exist before the ubiquitous PC and the enormous number of new PC owners. Many independent computer consultants today focus exclusively on serving the needs of PC owners. The PC consultant might be a software-development expert, an expert programmer, or a systems analyst. On the other hand, the consultant might not be familiar with any programming languages or mainframe systems theory.

The market overall for computer consulting has undergone revolutionary change in the past decade, and many new and different needs for consulting help have evolved. Today's computer consultant must specialize within his or her specialty in deciding what services to offer prospective clients. The choice of specialty may be influenced by happenings totally external to the consultant and his or her preferences, and are sometimes even chance occurrences.

As you meet the consultants who appear in these pages, you will see how often chance played a part in the individual's career choices. You will see something that is common to all consulting: The individual did not start out with any notion of becoming a consultant. That decision appears to be a spontaneous one, representing a change of professions or, at least, a change in the way the individual chooses to practice his or her profession.

The PC owner's needs

It is almost impossible to typify today's computer owner. The PC is both personal property—students use them for schoolwork and others for hobbies—and business equipment. Virtually everyone has a use for a PC.

The needs of an average PC owner, with regard to a computer investment of approximately $2,000 to $5,000 per PC are quite different than the owner of a mainframe that represents dollars in six or more figures. In general, you do not need to know Fortran, Unix, C, Clipper, PL1, or other sophisticated computer languages and operating systems to help PC clients who need support. For the most part, they are using off-the-shelf software bought from local computer retailers, and most of these are relatively easy to learn and operate. Still, there are many programs complex enough to justify special training of users—spreadsheet and database programs, for example—and even simple, easy-to-use programs and devices need to be installed to work smoothly with other hardware and software.

The computer industry is still in sore need of improvement in writing skills, in the menus and "help" programs that appear on the screen, as well as in the owner's manuals. Many PC users still find installing new software programs an intimidating task and retain consultants to help. Too, most programs are upgraded or improved periodically, and the improved version of a favorite program must be installed anew.

The pages that follow explain the business side of establishing a successful (and profitable) business from your home.

"Worthless."

—British Royal Astronomer Sir George Bidell Airy
  characterizing, in 1842, Charles Babbage's
  Analytical Engine, acknowledged as the
  forerunner of the modern computer.

1 Defining the home PC consultant

We are still largely a computer illiterate society. Most people, even those who have learned certain tasks and use computers daily for those tasks, remain in awe of the machine and technology. They resist learning more than the minimum necessary to their immediate needs. Most PC owners are not technicians or "power users." They have no time or desire to become experts; they look to PC consultants to help them when they encounter problems.

These are your prospective clients, and their needs are many, as are your opportunities. Your own need for specialized expertise as a consultant is relative: "in the land of the blind, the one-eyed man is king." You need not know everything there is to know about PCs. Indeed, as a home-based consultant, you probably don't have the resources—in time or money—to do so.

Because of the enormous diversity of PC uses and needs, there is no single set of qualifications necessary to be a home PC consultant. The requirements depend entirely on what services you wish to offer. That list of services usually determines what kinds of clients you will pursue, but the inverse may sometimes be the case: you first select the kind of clients you wish to serve, and then determine the services they need.

Qualifications: What does it take?

In the pre-PC era, computer consulting was concerned almost entirely with software matters. Even today, the ability to write programs is the most common characteristic of computer consultants, although it is a skill that varies widely, from relatively simple programs to complex programs written in highly sophisticated computer languages. However, the number and diversity of computer services has grown with the number and diversity of computer owners. As a home PC consultant not attempting to provide every possible service to everyone who owns a computer, you need not master all computer-based skills. You need not even be a programmer. You might, in fact, have any or all of these backgrounds:

The computer hobbyist   Many computer hobbyists are as expert as trained and experienced computer professionals. (In fact, hobbyists tend to be far ahead of the professionals in their enthusiasm and zest, which often more than compensates for their relative inexperience or lack of formal training in computer sciences.)

Many of the talented pioneers in the personal computer field were hobbyists, including Steve Wozniak and Steve Jobs, founders of the Apple Computer company and prime movers in transforming the new novelty into a serious new business entity when few others were taking it very seriously. Just as interesting is the background of Bill Gates, head of his own company, Microsoft, another young mover and shaker of the early PC days.

In the PC world, your knowledge and abilities are still far more important than your status as a professional or nonprofessional computer specialist. In fact, many successful independent computer consultants discount the importance of formal education.

Experienced programmer/system analyst   Despite the many exceptions, most computer consultants have good programming skills and many are also qualified system analysts. Surveying the biographies of a number of PC computer consultants, I found that most did have some programming background and many had experience in higher levels of software work, such as system analysis. At the same time, I have also found that many experienced software professionals no longer do software development as consultants, but offer other services that are equally important to the clients. Thus, software development skills are an asset, but not a necessity to the practice of consulting in the PC arena.

Experienced computer technician   A good knowledge of PC electronics and the various models, configurations, and accessories of computers is one basis for a PC consulting practice. Such a capability enables you to offer computer maintenance services of several kinds, including troubleshooting, repairs, component replacement, the addition of accessories, and advising clients in these areas, as well as guiding clients in the choice of computers best suited to satisfy their needs.

Graduate in computer sciences   While many PC consultants have college degrees, many others do not. Moreover, even among those who had college degrees, quite frequently the degrees were in fields unrelated to computers. David Labell, an independent computer consultant working from his home in the suburbs of Washington, DC, was a Liberal Arts major with a great interest in religion before he became enamored of computers and decided to seek a career in that field. He then went back to school to take courses in computer sciences and programming, although he says his mastery of programming is mostly self-taught, something one hears from many computer consultants.

A degree in computer sciences might provide you an advantage over some of your competitors, and is certainly an asset, especially if added to some practical experience. (I did find that some consultants had little industry experience, but went almost directly from college to independent consulting.)

Computer or electronics engineer   Many electronics engineers have turned to computer consulting, often to the software side rather than the hardware side of the field. Either way, the educational advantage of the formally trained graduate engineer is a considerable asset in both absolute knowledge and in professional credentials.

Martin Schiff is a PC consultant working from his home in Maitland, Florida. His father was a general contractor, and Schiff started working for his father in the construction business. He remained in the business until his early thirties, when he decided that he was not in love with the construction business and did not want to spend the rest of his life in it. By then, the company had bought its first computer, and Schiff began to learn how to use it, which led to a growing interest in computers generally. When he decided to make his career in computers, he began to stay up nights learning to program while he went to college for the first time to earn a degree in computer sciences, eventually launching himself into an independent consulting venture.

A few examples

Paul LaZar is a computer consultant in Silver Spring, Maryland with quite a different background and set of leanings. LaZar is an electronics engineer who started as a communications specialist, but soon decided that he was stifled working for big companies. He is by nature an inventor, and in the course of some of his early independent ventures, he began to develop an interest in computers and began to formulate some ideas of his own about what a desktop computer ought to be. That led him to go back to school at night to study computer programming.

In the early days of the PC, Paul built his "Generation 5" desktop computers for a variety of clients, including government agencies. Before long, he found himself building several different types of desktop computers for customers with different needs. As the dynamic PC industry continued to develop new and better designs, LaZar found himself asked to upgrade older computers. Then he found a need for training customers, and soon enough, as organizations bought more and more computers, he was called on to help them network their computers via LANs—local area networks—that linked them together and to common server devices, such as printers. As computer manufacturers proliferated and prices dropped precipitously, LaZar phased out the computer-manufacturing aspect of his business and reorganized his enterprise as "PAL Technology" to reflect a sharper focus on technical consulting. Today, he is pursuing what he calls "telecomputing," making more significant use of the PC's ubiquity and as yet relatively untapped capabilities.

Bill Rink, in southern California, is an electrical engineer who became interested in computer technology and learned to program through "OJT" (on-the-job training). Rink is oriented toward the newest and most sophisticated hardware, and consults on both hardware and software applications. "I do a lot of work with hardware development," he says, mentioning working with workstations. "At the moment, I am doing mostly design work with microprocessors and firmware." He mentioned also working with the development of medical equipment, and agreed that his consulting was involved in the high-technology applications of computers much more than in their business applications. He enjoys working with the developmental models and test equipment—oscilloscopes, meters, and other such tools—that such a focus requires.

John Parker, who offers a number of computer services in consulting as Megabyte Computer Services of Pontiac, Michigan, does not write programs. "I think maybe a few years back," he says, "programming may have been a necessity in this biz, but there are so many programs available now that one doesn't really need to write a custom program for each client. Sure, there are still going to be specialized applications that need special programs, but most of the small-size businesses I deal with can use the many commercial programs readily available. Should I run into one of those specialized applications, then I can job that out to a friend who does program."

Parker's practice is quite diverse. He offers to build computers to custom requirements, but also lists among his services such items as training, application programming, network installation, bulletin-board installation, and general support and maintenance.

This diversity of talents, backgrounds, and directions is typical. If there is truly an "average" or "typical" independent PC consultant, I have not been able to find him or her. The descriptions, orientations, characteristics, and backgrounds of independent PC consultants are as varied as are those of the general population.

How specialized must a consultant be?

It is as difficult to be a generalist within the computer field as it is in most technical fields today; consultants are compelled to be specialists, sometimes even within their specialties—in other words, to become highly vertical in their specialization. Many consultants list several specialties, but still do the bulk of their work in one specialty and think of themselves in terms of that specialty.

Martin Schiff, for example, says he works almost exclusively in FoxPro, thus specializing further within the specialty of database software maintenance and development. He says that he is not often called on to develop new programs, but does more maintenance programming than anything else.

Superspecialization of this sort is especially true of the self-employed computer consultant, whose diversification is limited by the necessity to do everything personally. Diversification may come to the consultant later, with growth, but by then the consultant has become a consulting company and is no longer an independent consultant!

Understanding how people use computers is prerequisite to understanding where and how to specialize—the many opportunities for selling services that owners of computers need. The PC today is on the desks of students and hobbyists in their homes, but it is also charged with the serious work of governments, businesses, industries, and other organizations of every size, from the self-employed individual to the supercorporation.

The range of PC users

The range of uses for the PC, therefore, is extremely wide. At one end of the spectrum, we have the PC owner who uses a computer at home to play games, read stock market quotations, do homework, "chat" with friends on electronic bulletin boards, write, take work home from the office, and otherwise use the personal computer as a hobby, a diversion, and a household utility.

At the other end, we have the established business or other organization that uses an entire population of the most advanced desktop computers for many of the business and professional purposes for which mainframe computers were once exclusively used.

Between these extremes is the small business, especially the work-at-home business, a rapidly growing entity, inspired, fueled, and made possible largely by the PC itself. More and more individuals are arming themselves with the business resources of computers, copiers, fax machines, and other utilities to set up completely capable businesses in their own homes. They are fast becoming a substantial economic force and a major market niche in themselves. Many, if not most, depend a great deal on their computers as a major asset in running their businesses, and so represent a market target for computer consultants.

The similarities and differences among these different types of users, and the markets they represent, is discussed in more detail in chapter 4.

PC consulting specialties

Many PC consultants specialize in designing, writing, and customizing software for clients. The clients for such services are usually fair-sized business organizations. However, there are many clients whose needs are far simpler, and they call on consultants for relatively simple tasks and services. Thus you can function as a successful PC consultant by offering basic and simple PC services such as the following:

- Advice and help in choosing computers and peripheral equipment suitable to clients' needs
- Advice and help in choosing software programs most suitable to clients' needs
- Setting up—installing—the hardware systems
- Installing software programs
- Advice and help in choosing supplies and establishing sources of suitable supplies
- Advice and help in upgrading hardware and software
- Installing local area networks to interconnect a number of personal computers as a single system
- Instructing users—training them—formally or informally
- Troubleshooting and solving problems

PC consulting involves more than PCs

Many computer consultants are computer technicians, probably software technicians for the most part, and usually very good computer technicians. They can install and even modify a client's equipment and software. They can guide clients through and train them in all the technological details of the hardware and the software: maintenance, repair, formatting, copying, erasing, and so on. What they cannot do, all too often, is show the client how to apply all these technological marvels to the practical problems of the client's business or profession.

The consultant as problem solver

The essence of consulting is coping effectively with unique situations and providing unique solutions. The ideal consultant is analytical, imaginative, inventive, and resourceful, but also understands the client's business or industry.

Consultants are inherently required to be problem solvers. It's in the nature of consulting, despite the fact that not all consulting tasks require it. Clients with problems expect consultants to be able to solve them, even when the client cannot define the problems. Asking a client, "What's the problem?" is likely to bring forth a recital of disappointment in the results, whatever they are—"It freezes up on me," or "I can't get it to double-space." Or you might get a description of some frustration (a symptom, in fact) such as, "I can't get the floppy disk drive to work," "I can't make sense of the printout," or "I can't find out how many hours I spent on each job."

As a consultant, you must learn to accept this kind of input gravely and go about collecting and analyzing symptoms to identify the problem. Don't expect more help than this from your clients, for you rarely get it. It's because the client is totally baffled and feels helpless to cope with the situation that he or she calls you in. But don't underestimate the need to define the problem. You are not likely to be successful if you do not determine precisely what the problem is. Accurate definition of the problem is a large part of the solution.

Your need here is not to develop technical knowledge adequate to the troubleshooting task; you probably already have that knowledge. You need to "pattern" your thinking. Problem solving begins with problem definition, and an accurate problem definition is itself a direct pointer to a solution. For example, when an acquaintance's new color monitor suddenly dropped all reds, he called his computer consultant.

"Just one color?" the consultant asked.

"Just the reds," the user answered.

"Check the plug," the consultant suggested.

The user did, and it was hanging partially out of the port.

Of course, most problems are not that simple. The problem-definition process has sequential steps (although it might seem to be immediate as the result of long experience). The first step is the statement of trouble or the apparent problem. Then comes the observation of symptoms and the formation of a hypothesis, followed by testing the hypothesis. If the test is not successful, you repeat the process, with a new hypothesis, and possibly an additional effort to gather and observe symptoms.

It is not by chance that so many consultants repair or improve existing programs far more often than they write new ones. Your diagnostic abilities are essential, but so is your knowledge of your client's business. Without both, you are severely handicapped in learning what to do, no matter how well you know how to do it.

The client who wants to build a customer database might understand marketing and even the more specialized field of databased marketing. He or she might thus retain a consultant only for help in the technical aspects of choosing and using a database management program. But suppose that client is not knowledgeable in databased marketing and wants help both in that technique and the necessary computer technology. The client then needs help in more than the technical details of building and managing a database file. He or she needs advice as to what belongs in the file, how to get the data needed for it, the many uses to which the database can be put to support activities, how to design it to support those activities, and what type of database file is best suited to the need. The consultant then must have at

The meaning of "application"

least some basic understanding of databased marketing to provide full and competent service.

The same considerations apply in many other areas. The client who wants to use desktop publishing software might need counsel on conventional publishing practices and the right kind of hardware and software, as well as in using the software. The client who wishes to turn to direct mail for sales support might need guidance by someone who knows that field of marketing, as well as what hardware and software is necessary and how to use it effectively.

There are PC litigation consultants, who assist lawyers in preparing and trying cases, even acting as expert witnesses. To do this on a regular basis, they must have a good knowledge of the legal processes and terminology in addition to computer competence.

Even the private citizen who uses a computer to help manage personal investments might need guidance from someone who understands investments and the stock market, as well as how to use a computer most effectively for investing.

In a debate among a number of experienced independent computer consultants, several made a sharp distinction between those who write pure computer software—operating systems, assemblers, and so on—and those capable of writing applications programs. Both call for computer programming capability, but the latter requires a good understanding of the application for which the software must be designed. But even that is not the only dimension to applications-oriented computer consulting. Martin Schiff pointed out that he had a number of years' experience in the business world—the construction industry, in his case—and this was a valuable asset for him, an asset that one does not get in formal education, but only through experience. Bill Rink also follows this course, and does most of his computer work in technology applications—state-of-the-art electronics and digital systems—where he has the greatest interest, knowledge, and experience.

Martin Schiff points out that there is programming and there is *applications* programming, and they are distinctly different from each other. You might design and write a database program in the abstract, but every client's needs are different. The client can tell you what his or her problems and needs are, but they will be in lay terms. You, as the consultant, are limited in what you can do to meet the client's needs if you do not have some understanding of his or her business.

Management consulting vs. computer consulting

The foregoing considerations put a different spin on consulting and the requirements for being an independent computer consultant. There are management consultants and there are computer consultants, but the need for combining these adds a new dimension. It opens the door to another spectrum of consulting still linked closely to computer consulting because it concerns how to use computers most effectively in the conduct of business and other activity, whether as a new start-up or as a conversion to computer equipment and methods. Understanding the client's professional or business application doubles the appeal and value of your services, as the lack of it handicaps you severely in delivering services of maximum value.

Management consulting is a broad term, virtually a catchall, as used by consultants. It's the term some of the major accounting firms such as Arthur Andersen use to describe their consulting activities, which are far-ranging and wide. They can be far-ranging and wide because these firms employ entire staffs of specialists and are thus prepared to advise in many fields. They can, because they have the diversity of staffs and capabilities, combine one or more computer specialists with one or more management specialists to constitute a multidisciplinary team.

As an independent consultant, you might at times find yourself in need of help, either because the total workload is too great for one person or because you need someone with special knowledge or experience. However, most of the time you must be your own team. Being required to supply more than one skill is not unusual in consulting, and is, in fact, often the key to success as a consultant. You must therefore narrow your focus as a computer/management consultant and try to combine the relevant computer skills and management skills in your line of services. If you are well-versed in both computers and some other field—especially in computers as used in some other field—you have a special capability, of which you ought to take full advantage.

Here are just a few ideas of the many fields to which you might add good computer knowledge to distinguish yourself as a special kind of computer consultant:

- Accounting
- Advertising
- Broadcasting
- Cartography
- Contract services
- Databased marketing
- Direct mail
- Inventory control and management
- Investment counseling
- Invoicing and collections
- Legal research
- Manufacturing
- Marketing
- Medical research
- Package design
- Printing
- Public relations

The one-person "team"

- Publishing
- Purchasing
- Sales
- Training system development and delivery

The list could go on almost endlessly, but the point would be the same. Almost every human activity can be computerized, but there are not enough specialists—consultants—who are equally effective in both the subject area and the relevant computer technologies.

Here, to illustrate, is a somewhat simplified example of what can easily happen (in fact, did happen in my own experience) when the consultant's knowledge is too closely confined to computer technology alone:

A company's comptroller meets with a computer consultant to discuss writing and installing computer software for a payroll system. (It is more likely that the comptroller would want recommendations on the most appropriate off-the-shelf software modified or customized to the specific application, but the principle is the same.) The comptroller is understandably not intimately aware of all the capabilities of today's computers and software, so he or she depends heavily on the computer expert's knowledge to help specify what is needed. The computer expert knows little of corporate accounting and other needs of the comptroller, so he or she relies on what has been done in previous payroll systems and in the comptroller's general explanation of needs. The result is a program that falls far short of what it ought to have been. In the actual case, the program ought to have included provisions to automatically monitor and calculate vacation time and sick leave earned, but it did not because neither party considered the need when discussing the program. Eventually, the client will call on someone to correct the deficiency or write a new program.

Creating a niche

It is not entirely accurate that there are not enough computer consultants who are equally expert in technology and the relevant business needs. There are simply not enough consultants who take *advantage* of their dual (and sometimes multiple) areas of expertise to increase their degree of specialization, even though this would add to their credentials and thus their value as consultants. Just as fledgling writers are urged to write about the things they know best, a computer consultant can benefit from applying computer skills to applications areas where he or she has experience and knowledge.

There is yet another way to create a niche for yourself as a PC consultant: Search out the applications for what you already know. Suppose, for example, that you are especially knowledgeable in spreadsheet software and its most sophisticated developments. Think about where the spreadsheet idea has its applications. But first think about the nature of the spreadsheet: What is it? What does it do? For whom does it do it? How does it do it? Why should anyone use it? (Is it superior to some older method or is there no predecessor for it?)

Finding answers to such questions often uncovers profitable niche markets that you have never before considered. Certainly the spreadsheet specialist who is expert at applying spreadsheet technology to the solution of marketing problems has a special value. There are spreadsheet consultants and there are marketing consultants, but the spreadsheet/marketing consultant is a very special breed not easily found.

Of course, as Mr. or Ms. Spreadsheet Consultant, you need not confine your specialization to marketing applications. You might also make yourself expert in using the spreadsheet concept for gaming and what-if projects (as the military often does), for inventory control, for product packaging, for advertising, and for dozens of other applications.

As software development approaches its zenith or, at least, slows somewhat in its sophistication, your future as a computer consultant lies far more in your mastery of applications as a viable business philosophy, rather than as pure computer-linked technical capability. If you rely entirely on your technical abilities, whether software or hardware, you are doomed to be a "me too" kind of consultant, struggling in the ever-widening sea of computer consultants. You will do much better to carve out a special field of your own.

If, for example, you opt to specialize in computer applications for accounting firms, you need not be a CPA to work effectively in the field, but you are certainly more effective and have more appeal to accountants if you have a good understanding of accounting practices and alternative systems. The mere fact that clients can talk to you in their own professional language is a great asset.

The consultant/client relationship

Among the problems of consulting is that of getting along with clients. Remember, both the individual who called you in for help and any other staff with whom you must work are the clients.

The client's staff sometimes presents a special problem in interpersonal relationships. In many cases, staff personnel are almost automatically hostile to consultants, whom they consider to be a threat to their own jobs. "Why else does management bring in consultants?" they reason. And if they do not consider you a threat, they might consider bringing you in to be an insult. For these reasons, the staff might be unfriendly, but more important, they might be uncooperative and make your job harder than it need be.

Be careful to do everything you can to get along well with the client and staff. The safest course is to be reserved and quiet; avoid "coming on strong" by all means. Don't try to make friends with staff people. If new friendships are destined for you, let them come naturally. Try to understand why your presence might alarm and offend employees, although this is not your fault, and be considerate of the employees' feelings. Be careful not to create any impression that you are there to teach them how to do their work, to correct their mistakes, to compensate for their shortcomings, or otherwise to represent anything more than another set of hands, doing the same kind of work they do.

The impression you make and the relationships you establish have a great effect on your marketing success, especially when it comes to winning new jobs from the same clients and winning new clients by referrals. You can hardly do wrong according to those who like you, and your work is rarely satisfactory to those who do not like you. The majority of computer consultants I spoke with observed that they got most of their new business by word-of-mouth referrals.

2 Getting organized

No matter how excellent you are at what you do, you must also be a realist: Consulting is a business. Proper planning and preparation go far in avoiding problems later.

It is an irony that as a home PC consultant you must be a specialist and a generalist at the same time. On the one hand, you must specialize in some functions and services related to personal computers; specialized expertise is inherent in the very idea of consulting. On the other hand, despite the fact that you are a specialist in what you do for your clients, you must also be a generalist in understanding and practicing a wide variety of business functions. This is inevitable because what you do as a consultant is not only a profession, it is also a business. Even if you retain other specialists for help with legal, tax, marketing, and other business concerns, you cannot completely escape the need to have some knowledge of accounting, pricing, marketing, customer relations, and perhaps even some other business functions.

Specialist & generalist

This does not mean that you have to be an expert in these other functions. You can pay for the services of lawyers, accountants, copywriters, and other specialists, and you probably will. They will carry out many chores for you—prepare the papers for incorporation, write your brochures, and make out your tax returns. However, often the most important thing they do is to advise you. They explain the situation and relevant factors, present their analyses, make recommendations, and describe their underlying rationales. But you must make the decisions. Even if your specialist recommends a decision to you, the responsibility for the decision is yours. It cannot be a wise decision if you do not have at least a working knowledge of the conventional business functions and understand the relevant considerations.

The question is, then, can you allow your hired experts to make or direct your decisions, or will you weigh the facts and make the decisions yourself? To do the latter, as you should, you must somehow acquire the necessary working knowledge. Hence, the need to become a generalist in terms of operating a business.

You will get some basic coverage of these subjects here, but space does not allow for more than limited discussions. My chief purpose is to make you aware of your needs in these areas and inspire you to do something special about them, such as doing extended reading and attending seminars or special courses. Many community colleges offer seminars and courses for small business owners today, and the associations you join might offer them too. However you acquire this business knowledge, it is an important factor in your eventual success. You will be able to do many business chores for yourself, if you wish to, but even if you retain others, you will be able to communicate well with them and to weigh and evaluate the advice you are given.

Roadblocks to success

Success is rarely easy to achieve under any circumstances and for any enterprise. The U.S. Small Business Administration, Dun & Bradstreet, and others claim that inadequacies in accounting, inventory, financing, and management are the general causes of business failure. In the case of the independent PC consultant, I have identified eight common and well-recognized obstacles that are serious impediments to success:

1. Insufficient starting capital
2. Restrictive zoning laws
3. Difficult licensing regulations
4. Difficulty in winning first clients
5. Limited number of markets
6. Prohibitively high costs of marketing
7. Inadequate personal credentials
8. IRS and other government restrictions

That these are common and well-recognized problems does not mean that all apply to you. In fact, it is unusual that anyone suffers from all these problems; it is quite enough to suffer from only one or two. In any case, let's examine each for possible solutions.

Start-up capital is a problem for many independent PC consultants, and yet it ought not to be, because little up-front investment is normally required. One of the more attractive features of independent consulting is that inherent in the very idea of consulting is the fact that the chief commodities are your already existing expert knowledge and skills. Most fields of consulting do not require any substantial start-up capital, other than that with which to support yourself during the time you are getting established. Even that might not be necessary, with careful planning and preparation; many independent consultants begin their practices with their former employers as their first clients. **Starting capital**

It is easily possible to invest heavily in a consulting venture, but it is not necessary to do this in the beginning. Instead, start with moderate start-up costs and invest only later, as business justifies it. Your principal stock-in-trade is your knowledge and imagination, and the delivery of the product is verbal, words on paper, or bytes on disk, so you do not require a significant inventory.

Many home PC consultants start in their spare time, while still employed, while still single, or otherwise equipped to survive early poverty. Others have help of one sort or another. Martin Schiff started on the proverbial shoestring, but had a wife whose salary as a chemical engineer helped him over the early days of his new practice. Paul LaZar is an adroit individual who probably did not need a great deal of help at any time, but it does not hurt that his wife is an accountant with her own practice, with hardware and software support supplied by LaZar. Harvey Summers, an independent PC consultant in Columbia, Missouri was among the first in Columbia knowledgeable enough about computers to help others, so he quickly acquired a huge reputation and had no problem finding clients. They sought him out, and he has since gotten his work primarily through word-of-mouth referrals. Most people are not as fortunate as Summers, however; it's a good idea to have enough start-up capital to support yourself for at least the first three or four months.

There might be zoning laws in your town that prohibit your conducting business in your home. However, the definition of "conducting business" can vary enormously. It might not apply to professionals who work at home, especially those who do not receive clients there. **Zoning laws**

On the other hand, some communities have strict zoning laws that are archaic and unenforced, but are never removed from the books and are technically still in force. In such cases, the authorities will not bother you about keeping an office at home, as long as you have no signs, no visible business activity, and no complaints from anyone.

In general, if what you do as a consultant does not require you to receive more than an occasional client at home, does not generate other traffic (many deliveries and pickups), and does not create noise or some other form of nuisance, you can keep your office in your home, as far as the law is concerned.

There are three possible remedies for a zoning problem. One is to avoid the problem entirely by renting space for your office in a commercial location. Another is to apply for a *variance*, a lengthy process that can delay your start for a long time and might result in refusal in the end. Still another is to anticipate the possible zoning problems and take steps that would give you a basis for arguing your case successfully, if need be.

Steve Wilson, a home-based consultant in Lansing, Michigan, had problems with the authorities because a disgruntled neighbor complained that he was in violation of zoning codes. He was able to satisfy the authorities that he had not violated the codes by arguing that he kept a post office box as his business address and never received clients at his home or advertised his home address, and thus his home was not used to conduct a business. That satisfied the authorities in his town and solved his problem. (Complaints by neighbors, although often for petty personal reasons, are a major cause of zoning problems. Many authorities will not enforce antiquated zoning laws unless someone files a complaint.) Check your own state and local government statutes. One respondent to a query I circulated on the subject reported that in Vermont, a state law blocks local zoning commissions from prohibiting home-based occupations, although local governments may regulate them to avoid traffic, health, and safety problems, and to ensure that the primary use of the dwelling is residential, by limiting the amount of space that can be used for business purposes.

Licensing is sometimes linked to zoning. A consultant reports that when in Albuquerque, New Mexico, she had no trouble getting a business license for her home. A friend in a nearby small community had to get her community board's approval, which she did by first talking to all her neighbors. She is now in Washington state and living in an area termed "rural" by the local government, where home businesses are the norm and are encouraged.

Licensing regulations

Licensing regulations tend to fall into the same pattern of possible difficulties that zoning laws do, except that few communities have any special licensing requirements directed specifically at computer consultants. In most cases you need only the typical mercantile and resale licenses, but it does pay to check on this with others to be sure that you have applied for the proper licenses. Be careful, however; you can run into unexpected problems. On one occasion, when I applied for a license I needed to do business in Miami, the clerk advised me that it was near the end of the license year and I ought to wait until the new license year started to save on fees. He assured me that it was all right for me to operate without a license in the interim. (In fact, as a WWII veteran, I was exempt from the fee, although I was still required to get the license.) However, a competitor complained, and I was summoned to appear before the authorities. Fortunately, the license clerk remembered advising me to wait and so the case was dismissed. Otherwise, I could have been fined rather heavily.

In some areas, licensing bureaus do not care where you conduct your business—they do not concern themselves with zoning restrictions—but in many cases, the two problems are tied together. You have to find out what the relevant laws and regulations are in your own state and community.

Winning your first clients is part of your marketing problem, as are the next two items on the problem list: limited number of markets and high costs of marketing. Winning those first clients is an especially important problem, since prospective clients often ask for the names of other clients to use as references.

Clients & markets

Many consultants win their former employers as first clients and often have such an arrangement in place before leaving their jobs. Martin Schiff says he won his first client, for a substantial $4,000 first project, by advertising on the bulletin board at his college. (He had never been employed by any company as a computer specialist of any kind, so he was not in a position to seek a first contract with a former employer.) Many computer consultants reason as beginning writers sometimes do, and accept first assignments for little or no money to get some experience and credentials (former clients as references) to support their marketing efforts. See chapter 4 for more on clients and markets.

The adequacy of your credentials as a computer consultant is essentially a marketing problem. IRS and other government restrictions are a special problem that have mostly to do with marketing also, since their chief effect is to hamper your status as an independent contractor in selling your services. These are discussed in detail in later chapters.

Credentials & the IRS

There are both major and minor details to consider in planning your venture. Some are essential to success, while others are purely arbitrary and neither right or wrong nor good nor bad. Before getting into a detailed discussion, however, it will probably be helpful to point out the several most essential matters that will make or break your venture:

Important decisions

- Developing a business plan
- Choosing a structure and name
- Marketing
- Pricing
- Controlling costs
- Accounting
- Legal issues

Do you need a business plan?

The very term *business plan* is a formidable one, and many business plans are indeed highly formal and formidable documents. Those are usually the business plans written about and in support of start-ups seeking big bucks for major undertakings. One cannot capture the interest of a banker, venture capitalist, or investor without such a plan to demonstrate the viability of the proposed venture and the soundness of a loan or investment. Thus, the writer of a business plan often starts from the assumption that it is to serve as a credential to support a quest for capital. In fact, the very term *business plan* is often a synonym for loan application or loan proposal. This type of business plan goes into matters that are irrelevant to the successful conduct of the business. It focuses, instead, on such matters as the ability to repay loans, the existence of capital assets, and other items that may serve as collateral to minimize risks to lenders and investors.

There is another type of business plan, which has as its purpose increasing the probability of business success by carefully planning financing, marketing, production, and all other operations in all departments of the business. Even if you have no need to raise capital for your practice, the development of this type of business plan is a wise move.

Of course, a good business plan can serve both purposes: developing front-end financing and setting standards and methods for operations. In fact, the business plan designed primarily to support raising capital must usually be far more detailed and exhaustive. It will normally have to survive rigorous scrutiny by lenders or investors (depending on whether you are seeking debt or equity financing), both of whom are quite cautious and methodical. Thus, it must cover all operations quite thoroughly. The existence of highly detailed planning, explained in detail, suggests strongly that you know what you are talking about. The more detail you supply, the more credible you appear.

As an independent consultant, you are undoubtedly quick-witted and resourceful, so you might manage quite well to build your ventures by "winging it"—marketing in spontaneous reaction to needs and opportunities as you perceive them and otherwise solving problems and finding solutions as you go. That kind of business insouciance is becoming increasingly difficult to achieve, however, even for the most quick-witted and resourceful among us. Success depends more and more on careful and detailed advance planning rather than on risk-taking.

Launching and operating an independent consultancy normally does not entail significant inventories, equipment, or other substantial capitalization, initially or later. The typical business plan required by the independent consultant is therefore primarily to satisfy the consultant's need for reference and guidance, although it should not ignore possible financial needs as well. In any case, it should serve as a map, pointing your way for development of the venture and providing checkpoints to verify that you are still on course.

Ideally, you should prepare it before launching the venture, but if you have started your practice without a business plan, it is not too late to develop one.

You can find many books and even computer programs about writing formal business plans. Most are written from the premise that the goal of the business plan is planning and financing the major venture. However, I will assume here that you are a one-person, independent consultancy, so your business plan should focus on the essential needs for start-up and operation.

The approach to your business plan

Many programs and books on the subject of developing business plans are available. One software package to try is Success Inc. from Dynamic Pathways, which also shows you how to plot the expansion of an existing business.

Some of the outlines found in these programs are quite broad, while others are minutely detailed. They call for listing a large number of things in setting objectives, goals, and bounds of the typical business plan. For the independent consultancy, it seems to me many of these more ambitious plans are a bit overblown. Your business plan is a document for your own eyes; you will probably never have an occasion to show it to anyone else, unless you are seeking financing or partners. Thus, it need not be too formal, but only suitable to serve as a guide and as a reminder to you.

Why a reminder? Perhaps you have heard the saying that it is difficult to remember that you started out to drain the swamp when you find yourself up to your bellybutton in alligators. Under the pressure of schedules and other stresses, it is easy to forget some of the things you started out to do, your main mission and objective. Thus, your business plan is a message from you to you, from the calm, methodical you, planning carefully and thoughtfully, to the overburdened, under-pressure you, trying desperately to stay on course, despite the storms.

Never forget for a moment, though, that your plan is based on estimates, not chiseled in stone. Try from the beginning to view the job of writing your business plan with that in mind. It is a draft, probably a rough draft, that will require many stages of refinement. Outline it in advance, if that is the more comfortable way for you to do it, but the real point is not the outline nor even the finished document itself: Writing the plan, in any form, forces you to think about what you must do, while noting alternatives, making choices, and making contingency plans. (The latter is too often neglected by those indifferent to Murphy's Law.)

I can suggest approaches, policies, and procedures here, but I cannot presume to solve your problems or make your choices for you; only you can do that. You must write the plan for yourself, and you must modify it too, from time to time. Review your plan periodically and see how well you have anticipated or estimated things. You are likely, to find that you have not always calculated or anticipated accurately, and your plan should be revised accordingly.

Finally, I am going to presume that you are still in the planning stages, preparing to launch your consulting venture. If you happen to be already launched into your practice, it will do you no harm to review what you have done or could have done about these things in your start-up. You might get some useful new ideas as a result. In any case, business plans usually must be reviewed and updated periodically, and perhaps this is the time to do so.

Business plan outline

Although I have proceeded here on the basis that you do not need a formal or rigidly structured business plan, you might prefer to use an outline form: It is a help in thinking things out because it enables you to view functions and their alternatives. Therefore, I am going to offer you a most generalized, simplified outline. Use it or not, as you see fit, delete what does not fit, and embellish it, edit it, or do whatever you wish to do with it. Most importantly, make it fit your needs, and your needs only.

Business plan

The company
  When formed (or when to be formed)
  For what purpose (describe briefly)
Organization structure
  Sole proprietorship
  Partnership
  Corporation
  Management
    Experience
    Strengths
    Weaknesses
Service(s)/products
  What are you selling?
  What makes it better/unique?
  Is it proprietary?
  At what stage is its development?
Comparison with competition
  Cost
  Quality
  Others on the market
  Description
  Current/estimated size (basis for?)
  Recent growth (sources?)
  Projected growth (sources?)
  Estimated market share
Markets to be pursued
  Planning to create new demand?
  Anticipating new demand?

Responding to presumed existing demand? (sources?)
Niches?
Marketing strategy
  What will service do for clients?
    Reduce costs
    Improve efficiency
    Produce profits
    Other
Pricing strategy, relative to market
  High, medium, or low?
Advertising and public relations
  Media
  Direct response
  Seminars
  Public speaking
  Association membership
  Newsletters
  Articles in journals
  Networking
Financial
  Financing sought?
  Why? (what purposes?)
  1-, 2-, 5-year revenue and net income projections
  Projection of when profits will begin (number of years)

Choosing a structure

In order to develop your business plan, you need to decide how to organize your business. Assuming that yours is to be a one-person venture (at least in the beginning) rules out partnerships. That leaves you with the choice between sole proprietorship and incorporation. Let's look at some pros and cons of each briefly.

Sole proprietorship

To operate as a sole proprietor, you don't need to do anything special. Every commitment you make is your personal one; you are self-employed, solely in control of everything, and solely responsible for everything.

That is both good and bad. It is good to have complete and total control, but there is a drawback in being solely responsible for everything that transpires as a result of doing business. We live in a litigious society: lawsuits, even groundless ones, are expensive, both in dollars and time. Some lawsuits can mean that judgments against you are awarded, and those can be applied to your personal property when you are a sole proprietor, jeopardizing your home, your automobile, and other personal assets. For this reason alone, many independent consultants opt for incorporation. But there are other reasons for considering the corporate organization as your business structure.

Incorporation

It is quite easy and inexpensive to incorporate in most states. In fact, many states provide a simple, one-page form as an application for incorporation, with a fee of less than $100, even as low as $50 or thereabout. In most states, you apply to the Secretary of State or the equivalent official, and you need to do nothing more than fill out the form and remit the fee. And wait.

There is a waiting period in which a search is made to see if there is an existing corporation using the name you have chosen. You can choose any name you like, but if you choose something like "Ajax Corporation" or "XYZ, Inc." there is an excellent chance that there will be such a corporation already, and you will have to choose another name. You can incorporate your own name—"John Jones, Inc."—but if yours is a common name, you might run into the problem of another John Jones having already incorporated his name. Try, therefore, to choose an individual name. I chose to be "HRH Communications, Inc.," and found no one else using that name, fortunately. It was not only distinctive, but was general enough to serve as a vehicle for a variety of services and products.

If you have the common notion that you gain instant prestige with prospective clients, suppliers, and bankers as a result of incorporation, disabuse yourself of that idea. Incorporation does little for you in that regard because anyone can incorporate quite easily and inexpensively. If you want to incorporate, do so for the right reasons.

Incorporate in the state where you do business (presumably your home state). If you are incorporated in a state other than the one in which your business is based, you will have to register as a foreign corporation, which means additional fees and complications.

Incorporation shields you from endangering your personal property if someone sues your corporation successfully. That doesn't mean that you have a blanket immunity, however. The "corporate shield" can be pierced if you are guilty of wrongdoing. Officers of a corporation are responsible for operating the corporation totally within the law.

While incorporating affords you a good bit of protection, it also means adding new problems. Most states levy added taxes against corporations, and your tax returns become more complex. This is offset by taking advantage of your corporate status to grant yourself benefits in lieu of salary that reduce your personal tax liability. Confer with a good CPA, and possibly a lawyer, if you incorporate to get expert advice on how to use the corporation to your greatest advantage.

I have always thought that most people venturing into their first enterprise agonized much too much over the "trivia" of business, including the business name. What real difference does it make if you trade as "Joe Jones" or as "Great American Management Information Associates?" Are prospective clients discouraged by the first name and inspired to confidence by the latter?

In fact, pretentious names such as that latter one can backfire. One executive I know who buys technical and professional services regularly is amused by elaborate business names. He chuckles when he gets a brochure with such a name and murmurs, "The smaller the company, the bigger the name." He long ago noted that some very large and successful corporations had fairly simple names to begin with—Radio Corporation of America, General Electric Company, and International Business Machines— and then simplified them further to RCA, GE, and IBM, respectively.

The real point is to have an objective by deciding what you want your name to be or do for you:

Be impressive   Trying to make your business name impressive is a vain effort and a bad idea at best. It is unlikely to impress anyone and is likely to become a burden to you in more than one way. Simplicity is never in bad taste, and understatement is often far more impressive than hyperbole. I am constantly dismayed, also, by beginners squeezing out many dollars they cannot afford to commission the design of a logo to which no client or anyone else will pay more than passing attention.

Be distinctive   A distinctive name is a good idea, if you can hit on one that is dignified, is relevant to what you do (preferably, to your PC specialty, rather than to the PC in general), and is not excessively long or pompous.

Be easy to remember   This is a valid objective for any business, especially one in which you hope for business via word-of-mouth—i.e., having clients seek you out.

Be definitive   Choosing a name that is definitive is also a meritorious objective, and probably the most important one. Forget about being arty and cryptic; prospects will not be impressed nor attracted. They are busy business people who need to get things done. They will understand "Computer Training Associates," but will be puzzled and probably not amused by "Ones and Zeros, Inc."

If you incorporate, you do not have to do anything further to register your business name. If you are a sole proprietor, you have to register your business name if it is other than your personal one. That is, shall you be "Hannibal Horton, PC Consultant" or "Excelsior PC Consulting Associates?"

If you do business as Hannibal Horton (assuming that Hannibal Horton is your name, that is), you need do nothing more than get whatever licenses or permits your state and local government require. You can use almost any combination or variation you choose—"Hannibal Horton & Associates" or "Hannibal Horton PC Consulting Services"—but as long as you use your personal name, you need do nothing more in most jurisdictions. However, if you decide to become "Excelsior PC Consulting Associates" or even "HH&A, Inc.," you are using a *dba*—doing business as—name , and you will almost surely be required to register it. Registration is not an especially onerous or costly procedure; it generally requires filling out some forms and advertising that you, Hannibal Horton, are doing business as Excelsior PC Consulting Services.

There is a potentially great advantage in using your personal name as your business name. Quite often, the most effective marketing involves making your name well-known through your writings, public appearances, association activities, and other functions. Much of the benefit of doing these things—"making a name for yourself"—is lost when your business is named "Automated Management Data Systems, Inc." or some other such headline title. Consulting, especially by an independent consultant, is a highly personal business service, and it is very much in your interest to make your name as a consultant as well-known as possible.

Marketing

The success of any venture is not possible without marketing success, and with enough marketing success, almost any problem or handicap can be overcome or, if necessary, tolerated without serious damage. (The latter condition exists in many large corporations, as you might have observed for yourself.) Even so, marketing success produces business success only when sales are profitable, so there are some other matters of near-equal importance, such as pricing and costs.

The most important matter to be addressed by your business plan is marketing. Marketing—creating clients—is always the greatest challenge in business, and thus merits the greatest attention and effort in the business plan. The following are some of the most critical questions that are often neglected or overlooked when devising plans:

- What are you selling?
- What are your strengths?
- What are your weaknesses?
- What can you do to overcome weaknesses?
- Who are your real competitors?
- What are their strengths?
- What are their weaknesses?

There is extensive coverage of these marketing questions in other chapters, so it is unnecessary to dwell on them here. I tend to belabor these questions because consultants too often ignore or refuse to take the time to identify what they are selling, and to whom.

Pricing has an obvious importance. You must price what you sell within the limits of what clients will agree to and pay, but also within the limits of what you need to pay your bills and turn a modest profit. Being the cheapest place in town is hazardous to your business's health.

Many consultants seem to have great difficulty deciding on the rates they will ask, especially when they are starting a practice without previous experience. Beginning consultants constantly ask for guidance in this area.

How to charge?

One consideration that comes first is deciding what the most reasonable basis is for your rates. Many consultants charge a rate based on the time they must spend to get the job done. That might be an hourly or daily rate, and it might be based on an 8-hour day and 40-hour week, with premiums charged for overtime and for working on holidays and weekends. Others charge a flat price for the job. However, these are not arbitrary decisions. As Janet Ruhl, a Connecticut computer consultant, points out, unless you have the kind of experience that permits you to estimate the size of the job with great confidence in the accuracy of your estimate, agreeing to a fixed price for the job is risky.

On the other hand, most clients will not give you a blank check by agreeing to pay you for every hour or every day it takes you to get the job done. The client normally and quite understandably wants some control over costs. This is especially true when the client does not know you at all and has no idea whether you are highly efficient or otherwise.

Of course, many experienced consultants use both the hourly and fixed-rate methods of pricing a job, depending on the circumstances. Even if you prefer to work on the basis of flat, fixed prices for each job, occasions arise that call for hourly or daily rates. For example, a client might want you to provide general support for some indefinite period. You should have some set hourly or daily rate, even if you do not always price on that basis.

Which should you choose, an hourly or a daily rate? Or both? The nature of what you normally do might dictate which is the more logical choice. My own consulting normally requires some travel and some or all of the work on a client's premises, and is usually of several days' or weeks' duration, so it makes good sense for me to have a daily rate for most assignments. However, occasionally a client wants to visit me to get some information and advice, and wants to buy an hour or two of my time. In that case, I must stipulate an hourly rate.

In the Fall 1992 rates-survey issue of *The Khera Business Report*, a newsletter for PC consultants published by Khera Communications, Inc., hourly rates listed for a variety of computer consulting services range from a low of $15 to a high of $125. The averages for the consulting services surveyed are as follows:

- Custom programming (not database), $57
- Database programming, $55
- Documentation, $51
- Hardware and software reselling, $52
- Small business consulting, $54
- Systems integration/networking, $59
- Telecommunications, $55
- Training, $52

Asking a number of experienced independent computer consultants for their advice produces a wide range of figures, depending on the circumstances— the skill levels, the consultant's experience, and the location.

Obviously, there is not too much help here. We all want to earn as much as possible, of course, but we are constrained by market realities. To set a realistic rate, one that you have a reasonable expectation of having accepted by prospective clients, you must determine what the market is for the necessary service. That means finding out what competitors are charging and what clients will accept. The suggested rates just listed are probably all realistic within whatever conditions surround them.

In practice, you have to learn for yourself, through experience, what rates you can and should charge for your services. You might even have to have more than one set of rates, if you offer a wide variety of services.

You sell results

All of this is based on the presumption that you sell your time. Time is not really what you sell, however. As a consultant, you sell results. Suppose that three consultants address the same problem and all arrive at the same or equally satisfactory results. However, one requires 140 hours to do so, another requires 100 hours, and the third one requires 180 hours. If the third one charges $50 an hour, the job costs the client $9,000. The others, charging the same rate, would cost the client only $7,000 or $5,000. Three widely different prices for the same result!

The problem is deciding what is a fair price for the job. Is it $5,000, $7,000, or $9,000? Should the client be penalized because the consultant is slow (or perhaps relatively inexperienced), or should the consultant be penalized because he or she is highly efficient or experienced? There are no easy answers to these questions, but they do serve to point out the need to analyze the situation from more than the standpoint of the time you will have to spend in doing the job:

- How much skill or experience does the job require?
- How great is the benefit to the client?

- How much time and effort ought the job require?
- What is the market (locally) for such services?

Suppose, also, that you spend the time and money to take special courses or to buy and install special facilities that enable you to be far more efficient than ever in rendering your service. Must you sacrifice your own interests— i.e., must you do the job at, say, one-third fewer hours (and one-third less income) than would have been the case had you not made the investment? Are you not entitled to benefit from your investment, and write it off via increased income?

Of course you are entitled to recover the investment by increasing your profit margin. Was that not the reason you made the investment?

But suppose the reason you can do the job more efficiently than your competitors can has nothing to do with equipment or facilities. Suppose you made a different kind of investment by going back to school and acquiring some advanced knowledge that made you more efficient in some specialized area. Is that not an equally valid reason for earning more per unit of time? Of course it is. Your rates ought not to be *based* on time, although they might be related to it, but rather on results and the value of such results.

It is not easy to get answers to any of the questions about pricing. The amount of skill and experience required to do the job is your own best estimate, as is the amount of time logically required to do the job. The benefit to the client may be calculated in dollars and in time saved, but that is also your best estimate. What the local market is for your services might be the easiest of the questions to answer, but still difficult.

Help finding answers

The need to find reasonable answers to all these questions is a good argument for joining one or more local associations. Usually, such associations can help you find the answers. Belonging to a local computer club or belonging to several bulletin boards and online services can also be a great help in getting answers. Your own accountant (assuming that you hire one to handle your books and taxes) might be able to help you also, since he or she probably has other clients in the same business. In any case, it is not necessary to go it alone; there is lots of help available and it is available in many forms.

Even when that is said and done, and you have sought, solicited, and gathered the opinions of your contemporaries, it is your decision to make. You and you alone decide the worth of what you do for your clients. You and you alone decide whether you are worth $200 a day, $500 a day, $1,000 a day, or more.

There are tradeoffs. If you price at the low end of the scale, you will probably win more clients, perhaps every one you approach, and you will work more or less steadily. As you increase the rate, you will close fewer of your initiatives and work less, but you might earn just as much.

Costs Controlling costs (primarily overhead, but also other kinds of costs) is as important to earning a profit and surviving as is pricing. Every dollar of cost you avoid or eliminate equals an additional dollar of gross profits earned. In fact, you must have complete knowledge of those costs to fix your pricing structure adequately. Pay a great deal of attention to costs, and sort them out into categories:

- Costs that are fixed and (relatively) unchanging, such as rent or mortgage
- Costs that are variable according to circumstances beyond your control, such as gasoline, travel, and supplies
- Costs that are variable, but entirely under your control, such as advertising and entertainment

Most costs fall into these categories, and it can be important to have identified each class of cost in advance.

The Khera Business Report offers some broad guidelines for estimating costs:

- $50,000 for payroll
- $7,200 for rent
- $6,000 for equipment and furniture
- $5,000 for advertising and marketing expenses
- $3,600 for insurance
- $2,000 for accounting fees
- $2,000 for resources (books, magazines, membership fees, etc.)
- $2,000 for travel
- $1,200 for client entertainment
- $1,200 for legal fees
- $1,200 for office supplies
- $1,200 for telephone
- $1,200 for utilities

In this scenario, a self-employed consultant would have to gross about $84,000 a year to break even. As the report points out, "While the numbers in this example are not necessarily real, you can use the model to calculate a ballpark rate."

Accounting Accounting might appear to be a rather routine function that is not closely related to your success. In fact, the reverse is true. Accounting is of great importance in any business venture. It is necessary to know at all times whether you are profitable and, if not, where the problems are so that you can take proper remedial measures to cut losses and ensure profitability. You need this information to make sound management decisions—which services to continue, which to discontinue, and what rates to change.

Many programs, such as ACCPac, DacEasy, Peachtree, and QuickBooks, can help you manage your accounting and bookkeeping. While these programs can be quite useful, particularly for routine accounting functions, most require some basic understanding of accounting principles. They do not take the place of a good accountant, especially when you are initially setting up your consultancy.

We all need to consult with lawyers from time to time. In fact, lawyers are themselves consultants, although they do not usually use that term. Lawyers specialize, just as computer consultants do. Some practice corporate or business law only. Some specialize in litigation, cases in which they sue or defend someone being sued. Some work in criminal law, defending those accused of crimes. Some specialize in family matters, such as divorce. And some practice general law, which means they handle accident cases, divorces, contracts, wills, and other kinds of legal problems.

Legal services

There are lawyers who specialize in the legal concerns of those in the computer businesses, especially those who sell computer services and write and sell computer software. Among their concerns is, inevitably, copyright matters that affect computer programs. Thus, when you need legal services, you might have to seek out the legal specialist, just as your clients have sought you out as a specialist in your field.

You must understand that the lawyer you retain to help you is an *advisor*. He or she will render opinions and advice, but cannot make your decisions; only you can do that. Thus, ask for advice and ask all the questions necessary for you to make a decision, but never ask the lawyer to make that decision for you. That responsibility is entirely yours and most certainly should be.

This is not to say that lawyers advise only; they also perform a variety of other services where they do work, as well as advise, drafting briefs and other necessary papers. They do advise, but there are some who might not explain their rationales unless you ask for a full explanation, with all the pros and cons of the available alternatives.

Marianne Krcma (pronounced "kerch-ma") set up her computer consultancy outside of Baltimore as a self-employed sole proprietorship in the summer of 1992. Her company specializes in consulting and training in desktop publishing (DTP) software and hardware.

Profile: Starting up a consultancy

Krcma contemplated starting a consultancy for over two years before actually taking the plunge, even doing occasional moonlighting. The sudden "restructuring" of her job provided the catalyst she needed to try making it on her own.

Organization

In choosing a name for her business, she considered several possibilities, but ended up simply using her own name, sometimes with the description "Consulting Services" added. Because her last name is so unusual, Krcma provides a pronunciation key for it on everything she sends out—letterhead, brochures, and business cards. She recognizes the importance of making things as easy as possible for potential clients, "If they hesitate because they're afraid of mispronouncing my name, they might decide just to call someone else." Balanced against that problem is a high recognition factor: Once they've seen her name, clients don't forget it.

Krcma has a core group of six clients who provide most of her steady business, and several more who provide occasional work. One client is a former employer, the others were obtained through networking and, surprisingly, answering an ad in the Classifieds.

The typical services she provides for her clients include

- Training groups and individuals on Ami Pro, PageMaker, Windows, Word, WordPerfect, and other programs
- Writing macros and templates to help small businesses transfer files, standardize written communications, and produce marketing pieces
- Advising clients in the use of word processing and DTP technology
- Producing computer documentation and training materials

Finances & fee-setting

Krcma started her business with $3,000 of personal savings used for living expenses and startup costs—converting a spare bedroom into an office, upgrading computer equipment, and conducting a small, targeted direct-mail campaign. She consulted an accountant for help setting up her books and understanding taxes, but now handles the accounting herself. Because she is a self-employed sole proprietor with no employees or inventory, taxes are relatively simple: quarterly estimated federal and state income taxes, reconciled once a year, plus self-employment tax.

Although Krcma started out quoting an hourly rate for her services, she now usually sets fees on a per-project basis. She explains, "Most of my clients budget a certain amount per project, so it makes sense to fit my proposals to the way they do business. You have to be fairly confident in estimating your abilities when you bill by the project, though. Otherwise, you'll end up undercharging, a mistake I've made a few times." Billing by the project instead of by the hour is also one of the ways the IRS distinguishes between consultants and employees (see chapter 9), so it's a good idea whenever possible.

Collecting what is owed her has not been a problem for Krcma so far, although she has made a few "reminder calls." She attributes her low bad-debt expense partly to luck, partly to her close relationship with relatively few clients that simplifies recordkeeping, and partly to her ability to estimate accurately what her work will cost so that clients don't get hit with unexpected fees.

Krcma estimates that she will make slightly more money in her second year of consulting than she did as a full-time employee. In the initial months of her business, however, her income dropped by about 45%.

Plans

Krcma sets sales goals for her company each month, and keeps a careful eye on how well she meets those goals. "I've 'raised the bar,' I think, five times since I started," she recalls. "If I meet my sales goal two months in a row, I consider raising it."

Describing her consultancy as a "modest success," Krcma believes it is moving out of its initial survival phase into a period of growth. With that in mind, she is stepping up efforts to reach new clients by making sales calls to local businesses and increasing participation in business and professional organizations. She is also considering incorporation to provide some liability protection as her client list grows.

Her advice to prospective computer consultants: "Don't get into this just for the money. Unless you're exceptionally lucky or well known, it's not going to be there at first. Realize that, as a business owner, you have to make all the decisions, so find out everything you can about anything related to running your business. Read everything you can get your hands on: books, magazines, government pamphlets. Then, if you still want to, do it! Turning away from traditional employment was tough, but the freedom and variety is more than worth it for me."

3 Setting up your office

After you've got a business structure and plan, your next step is to set up your home office with the equipment and supplies necessary to run a successful consultancy.

Most computer consultants opt to work from their homes. It's a good idea for many reasons:

- It is the most economical way to get started.
- It helps you cut your personal expenses, hence the amount of personal income you must draw from your practice, by enabling you to write off some of your normal expenses.
- It eliminates travel time to an office elsewhere.
- It makes it convenient to work at odd hours and on weekends, which can be inconvenient and even impractical when your office is in another location.

However, working from home does not work for everyone. Following are some of the various considerations to take into account in deciding whether an office in your own home is practical for you.

Choosing a location

An ordinary office for a computer consultant requires about 200 square feet. A spare bedroom usually serves the purpose well, although many consultants convert a garage or a basement into an office, which usually provides a great

Space requirements

deal more space. (In my own case, we have a large, three-bedroom apartment and have converted two bedrooms for use as offices.)

Costs

A spare room at home is undoubtedly the cheapest and most convenient office space you can find. In fact, the cost is negative—represents a plus factor—in that you can write off part of your household expense and reduce your taxes by using your home for office space.

Taxes

The IRS permits you to write off the prorated cost of dedicated space in your home. That is, you can write off the cost of space used exclusively for business. Using your dining room table to sort mail does not entitle you to write off part of your dining room space, unless it is no longer your dining room but is permanently dedicated to business use. You may dedicate an entire room to business use, or even a portion of a room. However, if it is a portion of a room, you should erect a screen of some sort as a formal demarcation of the space for business use. On the other hand, you can share many other household and personal expenses, such as telephone, heat, light, insurance, and automobile use, with your business. To do that, you prorate the business use as some percentage of total use.

There has been a recent Supreme Court decision that makes it more difficult for many consultants to take a deduction for the prorated cost of space at home used as an office and place of business. The standards expressed in the decision are not absolute, but they concern whether the home office is the principal place of business. Unfortunately, the law, as written, uses that term, "principal place of business," and the Supreme Court struggled to find factors to weigh the question.

The test case was that of an anesthesiologist who kept an office at home. The Supreme Court disallowed his claim on the grounds that he did his work principally in hospitals and not in his office, so his office did not qualify as his principal place of business. Among the tests to be applied are how much time you spend in your office, whether you receive clients there, and whether you do there whatever it is you are paid to do.

If your office is physically separate from your home—such as a detached garage—there is apparently no question about its deductibility: It is automatically qualified. In time, we will gain enlightenment as to IRS standards in applying the decision.

Facilities & resources

Every business requires certain facilities and resources, in addition to a place to do business and a telephone. Some basic requirements that fall into these classifications are listed and discussed here. Some might not apply to you, of course, depending on the kind of services you offer your clients.

As a PC consultant, you will certainly need to have one or more computers with plenty of RAM and hard disk space. You will probably have to go a bit beyond that to set up a computer center in your office—adding a modem, business-quality printer, fax (either a stand-alone fax machine or a fax board), and perhaps other items, such as a scanner or plotter, if your practice requires them.

Your computer center

How much space, how much equipment, and what kinds of equipment you require and can establish as tax-deductible resources depends on the nature of your practice, of course. The IRS can call on you to justify all items for which you claim deductions.

Most consultancies require libraries. You can hardly carry everything in your head, and no one tries to do that, but relies on the logical alternative, the library.

Your library

The classic view of a library is that of books arrayed on shelf after shelf, categorized and classified. That view is a bit dated today, when books do not always materialize as ink on paper, but may be a cassette or disk that can project the information on a screen. That does not rule out the existence and justification of conventional books in a library, however. Most consultants still maintain an array of reference books that contain information needed to carry on their practices. For example, Marianne Krcma, the consultant profiled at the end of chapter 2, regularly uses

- The most recent *U.S. Master Tax Guide*
- Computer books on the software and hardware for which she does consulting
- Back-issues of computer, business, and design magazines
- Several collegiate dictionaries, editorial style books, and grammar books
- Business books about consulting, selling, and management

For administrative purposes, your library ought to be treated as an asset of declining value, since books do lose value as they age.

All physical facilities require furniture and, possibly, fixtures. An office needs a desk, chairs, a carpet, filing cabinets, and a bookcase as the minimum, but perhaps also a sofa and a few other refinements. You will have to judge for yourself what it will take to make your office completely viable as a base of operations for you.

Furniture & fixtures

The foregoing items are furniture. Another class of facilities are known as *fixtures*, which normally refers to shelving, racks, display stands, counters, and related devices. They are probably not necessary for you, unless you plan to establish a laboratory of some kind.

In any case, furniture and fixtures cost money, and money is one resource that is almost certainly in short supply, especially when you are starting out with a new venture. Thus it is wise to minimize these expenses in the beginning.

There are three ways to minimize these capital expenses:
- Buy the most inexpensive models.
- Buy second-hand furniture and fixtures.
- Use what you have at hand, even if you must improvise a bit.

I started in a spare bedroom, with an ancient, undersize desk, a tiny table, and a typewriter stand (for my copier) that I bought at a local hardware/do-it-yourself store.

Furniture-rental stores are an excellent source of used furniture and fixtures. Many cities have stores specializing in used office furniture. The classified advertisements of your local newspaper are also an excellent place to search for bargains, even in computers and other office equipment as well as in furniture and fixtures.

Marketing material

Use tasteful, not garish, business cards, stationery, brochures, and other such materials. Beware: It is easy to go overboard in an effort to be distinctive and impressive.

One consultant's stationery—matched business cards, letterheads and envelopes—that I saw not long ago was quite handsome, with the generous use of gold leaf on good-quality stock. Unfortunately, I had seen identical stationery in other offices and in the literature I received from the printer who offered this as one of his standard lines. Handsome and expensive as it was, it was not distinctive or impressive to someone who has seen it elsewhere.

Your cards and stationery can be quite simple, and yet distinctive by virtue of elegant simplicity. You can easily hire a graphic designer to create your "corporate look" if you wish, but make sure you can justify that expense. Find out what your competition is doing. If they have full-color, custom-designed logos, you should have one too. Otherwise, it might be unnecessary; a simple design on good-quality paper and card stock will do the job quite well.

You'll need at least one general brochure, printed in quantity to mail and hand out freely. It may be one of the small ones, printed on an 8½×11-inch sheet and folded two or three times, or it may be a larger size. It can be as inexpensive or as expensive as you wish to make it.

Of course, you don't want your brochure to be a shoddy affair. On the other hand, many independent consultants go a bit overboard in the hope of making their brochures impressive. There is a middle ground that is difficult to define in text, but when you survey the range of possibilities, you will be able to see what that mid-range is.

Avoid excessive verbosity and hyperbole in your brochure. They rarely pay off for anyone, and certainly not for the relatively sophisticated prospects you are likely to pursue. Use simple, straightforward language and rely on nouns and verbs to tell your tale, not adjectives and adverbs. Try to sound as factual as possible. For example, "I have documented 37 programs" sounds more factual than "I have documented dozens of programs."

Depending on what you do, one general brochure might not be adequate for your needs. If you are highly specialized—for example, you only train people in using database and spreadsheet programs—you can probably manage well with a single general brochure. If you offer diverse services— programming, writing, and training—you probably need at least three brochures, one for each activity.

Having several brochures can be important because people will pigeonhole you, no matter what you and your brochure say, if you do not take active steps against it. If they have used your services to write or adapt a few programs and then perceive a need for technical writing, they will go out and look for a technical writer. They will have decided that you are strictly a programmer.

The same thing happens when strangers read your brochure and it discusses your services in programming. If a prospect needs a trainer, he or she is likely to have already decided that you are a programmer and not the person he or she wants. Thus, you need a brochure for each of your specialties, if you offer more than one.

Memberships

Membership is an item few people think about in advance. Most industries and fields have their own collections of professional, trade, technical, career, and other specialized societies and associations who make common cause and seek means to help themselves by helping each other. It is usually helpful in starting and operating a small venture to belong to a trade or professional association or two. It puts you in touch with others who are in similar or related businesses, and out of such memberships often grow valuable business connections.

One organization of particular interest to home PC consultants is the Independent Computer Consultants' Association, or ICCA. The ICCA sponsors chapters in many major U.S. cities and holds a national spring conference. Among its benefits are a standard consulting contract form, client brochures, and several insurance programs.

Insurance

A major concern for many independent consultants and other small businesspeople is the problem of getting adequate group insurance for hospitalization and medical care. Those of us who are of ordinary means can't afford to be without such coverage for ourselves and our families, but individual coverage is too expensive for most of us. There are ways to get group coverage, however. One of them is via membership in a large association. Group health coverage is, in fact, one of the inducements to join such a group.

Along with health insurance, you might want to have disability coverage, a good idea for an independent entrepreneur with a family to support. You might be able to get that as part of group coverage also.

It is also important to have liability coverage. Although you might find it difficult to believe that you could do any harm to a client or prospective client, we do have a highly litigious society, which makes liability insurance desirable.

You should have typical fire and theft coverage on everything you own. If your office is in your home, you might be able to get this covered under whatever home-owners insurance you already carry.

For most of this insurance, I have found consulting an independent broker the most satisfactory way to get objective advice and guidance. If you have already joined a trade or professional association, inquire there first for recommendations. They might already have made arrangements for coverage of members on advantageous terms.

Contingencies

Even the best laid plans go astray, as we all learn sooner or later. The printshop owner is ill, so your brochures are not ready. The truck breaks down, so your parts do not arrive. The client's accountant resigns, so you don't get that badly needed check when it was promised. The list of things that can go wrong every day is endless. It is thus mandatory to factor in some contingency planning—some alternatives to fall back on. These fall into two classes: standard contingency plans for problems relating to normal, everyday operations, and contingency plans for special projects.

My own philosophy is to be as independent and self-reliant as possible. It's a bit more trouble and more demanding of your own time than using vendors for everything, and it doesn't save large amounts of money, but it isn't my purpose to save money. My purpose is to minimize the "Murphy's Law" hazards. Thus, I plan to avoid both the everyday problems that arise from the unexpected disasters and disappointments, and those that are peculiar to some project. Following are some examples of each category.

Contingency plans & preparation

I prefer to do as much of my own printing as possible, now that I am well-equipped to do so. I can't very well do a businesslike job of creating my own business cards, but I can create all the professionally correct labels I need, using one of the several excellent label programs available. I make and store all the labels I normally use, but I have the capability to make up any special labels I need.

I have a modem, a fax, and a copier of my own. They are the most economical models available, but they operate reliably, and they insulate me from many problems by furnishing instant remedies. When I was struggling to meet a deadline for a client in Puerto Rico, my fax was a savior: The client was able to send me page after page of information from Puerto Rico by fax, which I was then able to copy onto plain paper via my own inexpensive copier, getting a job done that would have been otherwise impossible.

For anything that is not totally and completely under your own direct control, a contingency plan is a wise precaution. If you use a mailing service to send out brochures and sales letters, be sure you have at least one other service available. Know at least two computer-repair shops, if you do not do your own computer maintenance. Use more than one vendor to scan documents for you, if you do that kind of thing regularly. Do business with more than one printer. Try to find vendors who will come to your rescue in emergencies— e.g., over a weekend or on a holiday. They can be lifesavers, in a business sense.

Sometimes you must depend on some outside service for something you do not ordinarily buy. On a few occasions, I found it necessary to arrange to have a printer to do a rush printing job for me. The first time this happened, the printer threatened to let me down at the last minute. He said he couldn't meet my schedule, despite his earlier promise to do so, and begged for extra time.

An example

I bluffed and said, "All right, give me my copy. I'll take it somewhere else."

He blanched and said, "If I can't do it, nobody else can."

I simply smiled at him and said, "It's not your problem, is it? It's now my problem."

Faced with losing the job, he backed off and managed to do the job in time to meet my schedule. But after that, I never had to bluff again—I always had an alternative prepared, and he never attempted that ploy again.

Always be prepared for Murphy's Law to strike.

4 Understanding markets & marketing

The market for independent PC consultants actually consists of many market segments. The numbers and diversity of markets for computer consultants is the most striking aspect of the field. The market continues to grow and to diversify, as does the dynamic PC industry in general.

Although PCs are over 12 years old, there is still the basic problem of computer literacy to overcome in your marketing efforts. For example, the manager of a multi-PC establishment might not know that the computers could be linked together to improve efficiency and save money. He or she does not knowingly have a need or problem, and is thus not a prospective client until he or she is educated a bit. A large part of marketing for PC consultants involves educating prospects about what you can do for them.

Computer literacy is a somewhat vague term that refers to something concrete—basic knowledge of computers and computer technology—but is undefined in terms of quantity. How much must an individual know about computers to be considered "literate" in the subject? No one can answer that question with any precision or confidence.

Computer literacy

In fact, the measure of computer literacy depends on the use one makes of computers. For example, I considered myself to be computer literate when I knew almost nothing about database management software. At that time, I had no need for a database management program. When I felt that need, I investigated the subject and learned what I needed to know about it.

Computer literacy, then, is perhaps best defined as the possession of that amount of knowledge that enables the individual to use a computer effectively for his or her own purposes.

One way many PC users develop and expand their computer knowledge is by joining computer clubs and attending meetings. The larger clubs, including the Capital PC Users Group, also run seminars and special-interest subgroups. Many also publish periodicals for members.

I joined such a club years ago, when I bought my first computer, and it was there that I became acquainted with a computer consultant (Paul LaZar, introduced earlier) who came to address us. (We were all recent buyers of computers, and most of us neophytes.) Later, I learned that LaZar had organized and was active in another computer club, and I joined that one too. Eventually, I (along with others who had become acquainted with LaZar as a result of his occasional visits to help us learn more about computers) became a customer when I found that he built computers under his own brand name and gave superb support to his customers.

Overcoming computer phobia

Computer phobia is, unfortunately, a common manifestation of those unacquainted with computers. Actually, I use the term *phobia* rather loosely here; the fear of computers is more an apprehension than a true phobia, I think. Whichever it is, it causes many people to shrink from acquiring even a modest degree of computer literacy. They have a fear of the unknown, especially something that they perceive to be mysterious and highly technical. They have a deep fear that they might press the wrong key or button and cause a catastrophe, despite all assurances that they cannot do any real damage by an inadvertent press of any key or switch.

You might think this fear works in your interest, in the short term, since it encourages the impulse in clients to bring an expert in to do anything that must be done with a PC. In the long term, however, this fear works against your interest, since it discourages the use of computers overall. When you encounter this kind of dread, try to help the victim overcome what is an irrational fear. It is in your interest as a computer consultant to help your clients develop a sense of comfort learning and working at the keyboard.

Identifying markets

I asked Harvey Summers, a PC consultant in Columbia, Missouri, what aspect or niche of computer consulting he had made his specialty. He told me that he had done a good bit of work in networks—LANs—at first, but was now concentrating on the multimedia market. He went on to point out that Columbia is a university town, in which education is the major "industry." Computers equipped with sophisticated sound and graphics boards and CD ROM drives are being used there to deliver education and training. It is obviously a fast-growing order-of-magnitude advance over the slide and filmstrip systems of yesterday, and even over videotape.

Summers is operating in the forefront of the technology, at least in one applications area. PC-based multimedia is a rather recent development that requires knowledge of the most up-to-date technologies. Many PC owners who could make good use of the technology probably are not even aware of it yet. The need for it can't exist if prospective clients are not aware of it, so part of Summer's job requires educating prospects to create the need.

That is bold marketing. The essence of marketing is satisfying needs, both *felt* and *created*. Most PC consultants, like other entrepreneurs, market to visible and easily identifiable felt needs of prospective clients. Felt needs constitute the bulk of the market and are worth considering first. Although we have already taken a brief look at the principal types of PC owners in an earlier chapter, we must now study those PC users from the viewpoint of a marketer—i.e., with a goal of identifying their problems and needs.

Rick Ross, of Liberty, Missouri, ran a PC consultancy in his spare time while working for a computer store and attending Missouri Western State for a degree in computer engineering. Ross began by helping computer buyers install their new systems and tutoring them in the basics of using computers. Later, when the store owners decided to offer installation service to computer customers, Ross found himself with a conflict of interest, and thus began his full-time computer consulting service. Today, he tutors clients in using their computers, but he also offers installation and on-site repair services. He counsels clients about buying their equipment as a free service, in return for handling their installation and tutoring.

There are millions of PC users, and the numbers are growing, partly because of the easy availability of computer-based services, partly because of the falling prices running directly counter to the inflationary trend, and partly because one has no choice, in many situations: most businesses, no matter how simple, need at least one modern PC. Rick Ross and many other PC consultants provide their services to small businesses, as well as to individuals who use computers in their homes.

David Gannon, operating his service in Newport, Rhode Island, is another consultant who caters to small businesses. In his own words, "I do computer consulting for small businesses—system specification, set-up, training, etc." Gannon started moonlighting as a consultant while in the Navy, and turned to full-time consulting when he returned to civilian life.

As a consultant, you basically sell a service of some kind, although you might also deal in related products. What you sell is determined largely by your desires and capabilities, but also by the demands of the markets available to you. You can't build a viable practice selling a service for which there are not enough buyers. A critical element of planning your consulting practice, therefore, is defining the market.

You must define your market in terms of who your prospective clients are, what their needs are, and which of those needs you can meet. That, in turn, requires you to find out what types of things PC owners do with their computers.

Many types of PC users

All PC users can be divided into three general classes:

- Individuals using personal computers for private and personal purposes
- Businesses using computers for a wide variety of business purposes
- Other organizations using computers for nonprofit purposes

The divisions are far from clear-cut, however. Some of the individuals are one- or two-person businesses, while "other organizations" use computers to do many of the same things businesses do. For the typical independent computer consultant, the best prospects for services are probably those who use computers for serious personal and business purposes. However, the markets are too diverse to make dogmatic assertions. All users and uses should be considered. The following criteria therefore reflect general truth, but there are many exceptions and areas of overlap.

Personal uses of PCs

For many, a PC represents a hobby or an avocation. It is useful for chatting with friends electronically via electronic bulletin boards, writing letters, doing work for school, and other minor tasks. However, many individuals own and use personal computers for more serious purposes, such as monitoring the securities markets, getting the latest news reports, and tracking down information of interest.

These users would ordinarily be relatively unlikely to use your computer services. The hobbyist especially would be unlikely to call a computer consultant, except perhaps if the PC requires repair or maintenance. Computer hobbyists are usually enthusiasts who become quite literate about computers and rarely require help from anyone. When they do, they are likely to turn to others, via a BBS (electronic bulletin board system), for helpful advice. Even in the event of a computer breakdown, the hobbyist's need is rarely so critical that he or she is likely to get panic-stricken and call for emergency help.

One part-time computer consultant reports being almost swamped by requests from individual PC owners for help with the simple tasks of installing off-the-shelf programs and instructing PC owners in such basic tasks as using word processors and communicating with BBSs. (He referred to the demand for such help as being "overwhelming.") He sees a large market for training and other help from this client population.

He reported charging only $25 an hour for his services, and remarked that it provided a welcome spare-time income. Experienced, full-time independent computer consultants were immediately skeptical that this was a practical approach or a market that would provide the basis for a successful practice.

The beginner's business naiveté was plain to them. Yet, there are ways to make even this kind of consulting practice pay, and in a later chapter we will discuss this and analyze the problem, with consideration of how to make money in even this market where the basic fee scales are rather low. (David Gannon reports that in Rhode Island, he finds his ceiling to be about $45 per hour.)

Businesses, including one-person businesses operated from home offices, use computers quite differently than do most individuals. Businesses use the computer to carry out normal business functions, so it quickly becomes an important, even critical, element of business. The cost of consulting services related to computers is then accepted as one of the many normal costs of doing business. Typically, computers are found in business offices today even more commonly than typewriters were a decade ago. It is not only the clerks and typists who have personal computers on their desks, but also the executives and professional specialists, who also use computers directly in carrying out their functions.

Business uses of PCs

Personal computers are used in connection with virtually all business functions, including personnel, correspondence, accounting, inventory, marketing, production, research, planning, and others. Once these functions are committed to computers as the media for their implementation, the computers and their functioning become absolutely essential to the everyday conduct of the business. The computers are the efficient servants of the business organization, but the organization becomes completely dependent on the reliable and efficient functioning of computers, mysterious as their operation is to the average user. Thus arises the opportunities for the able and dependable consultant.

Small business today includes the millions of modern home-based businesses, a segment that is growing rapidly. This is at least partly the result of the technologies that have placed personal computers, fax machines, copiers, telephone systems, and other high-tech developments into the hands of the tiny, home-based businesses, those enterprising individuals of modern times. (The House Small Business Committee once proposed establishing a class of "mini-small businesses," to distinguish the truly small business from the relatively large businesses now classed as small business.)

The home-based business

These home-based businesses are not modern-day analogs of the cottage industries of an earlier century. Those were based primarily on piece workers, laborers in a primitive kind of mass production. Today's home-office phenomenon consists of small but wholly independent ventures conducted in and from entrepreneurial bases in private homes.

The individual entrepreneur working from a home office is as dependent on his or her PC as are the larger corporations with their dozens or even thousands of PCs. The difference is one of degree, not of type. All businesses are prospective clients for you, although you are likely to find it more practical to pursue clients at one or the other end of the spectrum, rather than trying to market across the entire range of potential clients.

Many of those entrepreneurs who work from home and from small offices are not exactly "businesses," in one sense of the word, but are instead serious practitioners of one sort or another, such as physicians, architects, lawyers, and psychologists. They have the typical business needs of accounting, correspondence, research, and others, but many of their needs are rather specialized and not commercial in the sense of a manufacturing, sales, or retailing organization.

Other organizations' use of PCs

There are many other organizations that use desktop computers: governments at all levels (federal, state, and local) and their many agencies, labor unions, associations, community groups, schools and colleges, and non-profit groups such as HMOs (health maintenance organizations) and political groups. Surprisingly, on close examination, you will find that their needs are not unique, but are similar in many ways to those of corporations, professionals, and other PC owners and users.

Single-PC owners vs. multiple-PC owners

There is at least one significant difference between the needs of the owner-user of a single computer and the needs of a multiple-PC owner. The single-PC owner must have certain peripheral equipment, typically a printer and modem, at the minimum, but in some cases also a plotter, scanner, tape drive, Bernoulli box, and other devices. The owner of many PCs—a sizable corporation, for example—needs the same kinds of peripheral devices, but might not have each PC equipped with the devices. Instead, the PCs might be networked or linked to each other via a local area network and share the use of all those peripheral devices via the network. Thus the organization might have a dozen PCs, but be required to invest in only one laser printer, one plotter, and one high-speed modem. On the other hand, these organizations become even more dependent on the functioning of their LAN to keep all the PCs and peripherals operating effectively.

This alone represents a great opportunity for the PC consultant who wishes to specialize in LANs. Many PC consultants have done so, serving clients who have many computers in their offices or plants.

Common factors of all PC owners

All PC owners, except the hobbyists, have certain common factors. For example, all have marketing requirements. For-profit organizations have winning clients and customers—making sales—as their major marketing objective, but other organizations have marketing needs, too: associations, for example, market for new members. In fact, associations must practice marketing on a large and aggressive scale to be successful, often conducting seminars, symposia, conventions, trade shows, and other events. Colleges and universities also conduct seminars and trade fairs, or would do so if an imaginative consultant presented a plan and proposal to help them. Consulting includes imaginative and innovative thinking; modern marketing is not merely reacting to perceived needs, it is also taking the initiative to develop attractive ideas and programs for prospects.

Political groups market for votes and donations, and charities also try to win donors and pledges of donations. All are trying to win converts or contributors to their causes in one sense or another. Every organization has a mission, and computers can perform useful functions in helping each organization carry out that mission. One common computer use for all or most of these activities involves supporting related direct-mail functions. That means building, sorting, and managing databases. This is discussed in more detail in the next chapter.

Typical client needs

In general, there are two kinds of services clients are likely to need from you: one-time or occasional services, and continual or repetitive services. They fall into software and hardware areas.

Installing hardware

Installing a hardware system—hooking up all the interconnecting cables among the CPU, monitor, modem, and printer, for example—is usually a one-time service, one that might never be needed again or should logically be needed only when the client adds to or replaces the system. Troubleshooting malfunctions and applying corrective measures should also be characterized as infrequently required services.

Although most computers come with instructions and diagrams for setting them up for operation, first-time owners are characteristically somewhat fearful of doing it alone and turning on the switch for the first time. Many hire a specialist to do this for them and to instruct them in start-up procedures. In fact, they also want to be reassured that they know how to handle all the basic steps. Thus, installing hardware includes some training, a basic orientation to explain such terms as *DOS*, *boot*, and similar ones that even the novice must learn early in the game.

Installing software

Installing software is a different proposition than installing hardware. For a given program, it is a one-time need, but because most computer owners upgrade and acquire new and different kinds of software, many call on consultants frequently for help installing new software. In many cases, adding new hardware, such as printers, requires that the software programs be reinstalled to work smoothly with the new equipment.

Despite the great strides made in making software user friendly, many computer users have trouble—often based on fear—installing software programs. The installation processes for many software programs, especially large and complex ones, require the user to make decisions, such as what kinds of printers, monitors, and other software programs they are using, and how they wish to configure the program being installed, since in many cases there are many options possible.

Many owners eventually learn to handle their own software installation, but others call on consultants for the task. This is especially the case with large organizations owning a number of computers operated by their staffs. In many cases, they do not expect the users to be able to install new programs, but call on consultants for help in this as a matter of course, a routine cost of doing business.

Upgrading & modifying

As new chips are developed, newer, faster, more versatile, and more sophisticated PC designs evolve. At the moment, the 486 computer is state-of-the-art, although the Pentium is just over the horizon. Whenever a technological breakthrough is announced, PC users must decide whether to modify their existing computers or whether it makes more sense to buy one of the latest genre. Here, again, is an opportunity for the consultant to advise and, possibly, to actually upgrade the current computer.

Owners often want their computers modified to add new features such as tape drives, fax boards, and CD ROMs—or to add improved versions of these or other components. As desktop computers and accessories continue to evolve, the demand for such upgrades and modifications grows too, and represents business opportunities.

Modifications like these are likely to require reinstalling many of the software programs to operate with the new configuration—yet another opportunity for PC consultants.

General maintenance & repair

Modern electronic equipment, based on chips and low operating voltages, is far more reliable and long-lasting than the equipment of a few decades ago. At the same time, it is far more complex and sophisticated, with a vastly greater number of circuits and functions. Troubleshooting is thus often quite difficult, and calls for expert skills. However, computers have certain mechanical components (components with moving parts), notably the various drives, which are by their nature far less reliable than the electronic systems (which have no moving parts). Therefore, troubles and failures, both electronic and mechanical, do arise, and require the services of consultants. (It is probably fair to call computer repair technicians "consultants" because of the complexity of what they do.) Almost invariably, computer owners call for help in these cases.

One typical problem is hard disk crashes, which wipe out the hard disk as a working entity and requires immediate service. The disk must be replaced, but the data must also be salvaged, if possible. Ideally, most of the data would have been saved by daily backups, but that might not be the case. In many cases, the consultant is able to recover all or nearly all the data on the damaged disk.

There are other problems, more sophisticated ones, that require expert help, even when the PC owner is reasonably literate in computer technology. At least once a year I turn to my own computer guru for help, despite my relative independence in technological matters. I believe it is wise to turn to experts, and so do a great many other PC owners.

John Parker is an imaginative and resourceful marketer, offering a variety of services. Here is one described in his own words: "I have a maintenance service where I come in once a month and perform preventative maintenance on their computer. I check for viruses, defrag the HD, clean the floppy heads, etc. They can sign a six-month or a one-year contract. Naturally, they get a little taken off the price for a one-year deal." He reveals, also, that he is considering offering clients a retainer arrangement, with a monthly fee. He would then be always on-call for them, ready to come over promptly to take care of whatever problem they are having at the moment.

The need for knowledge of computers is another area of opportunity for the computer consultant. Training PC owners and their staffs can be done in several ways: seminars, direct methods such as OJT under your direct supervision, and through written materials. It can be done as a one-time general course, as a progressive series of sessions, or via some hybrid approach.

Training as a specialty

There is a vast market for training. Even with steady advances in such things as pulldown menus and help files to make programs easier to learn, the increasing complexity and sophistication of software has increased the popularity of training.

Almost from the beginning, word processing, replacing the typewriter, was the most common and most popular use of the PC. Many people consider word processing software difficult to learn. Many computer consultants, therefore, offer to train people in word processing programs (such as WordPerfect, for which there appears to be a large and continuous market). If you believe yourself to be expert enough in the use of some popular software, this is a potential market to consider as a specialty.

In addition to word processing, desktop publishing has become a popular computer consulting specialty, both doing it as a service and training others in it. Database management software, spreadsheet programs, and their applications are also growing, popular markets for computer consultants.

Information research and retrieval is another excellent subject for training services. One of the results of the computer age has been the storage of data in electronic libraries. One of these is MEDLARS, a huge database of medical information housed in Bethesda, Maryland in the National Library of Medicine operated by the Public Health Service. Another is ERIC (Educational Resources Information Center), a storehouse of educational research material. NASA has a growing database gathered in the course of its work in space and the many related sciences.

The average individual had no means to access these databases in the mainframe computer era. The PC has changed that. Public databases have sprung up, and they have proliferated rapidly because anyone with a PC, a modem, and a telephone can rent time on most of these databases and gain access to great stores of information on almost every subject known.

Lawyers, for example, can ring up Westlaw or LEXIS to find precedents and do other legal research without leaving their offices, as physicians can ring up MEDLARS or MEDLINE. Businesspeople who sell to the federal government can turn to CBD Online, a public database that provides daily information on government procurement—what the government wants to buy and where to get the solicitation packages, as well as notices of awards made and other procurement information. There are hundreds of such services today, and many PC owners need help learning to use their computers to do such research effectively and efficiently.

Users pay for the time they are connected to these databases, and connect-time charges can mount rapidly if they grope blindly. Using the public databases with a minimum waste of time requires understanding in advance just how the database is organized, how searches are conducted, and how charges are made. But even before that, users should identify, as specifically as possible, just what the desired information is. They can then formulate a specific search strategy before undertaking the actual search. This can be the subject of training seminars for clients who plan to use public databases.

Training is therefore a sufficiently broad field to serve as a basis for PC consulting in itself, or it can be just one of the services you offer.

Initial markets

Many beginning independent consultants see as their natural market the broad one they have seen as an employee of some large firm. It might be that you know only the general market in which your employer or former employer operates, and thus that is the only market you plan to address.

That might or might not be a good idea. On the positive side is the fact that you (presumably) know that market and probably know many people in it. On the negative side is the temptation to pursue, as clients, the clients you have come to know working for your former employer—in most circumstances, an unethical idea. Another negative aspect is that the market is probably too broad for you to address properly. It is far better, usually, to find some market segment or niche suited to your purposes. Remember that you are a consultant, and therefore presumed to be a specialist. Focusing on a specific segment is appropriate to that philosophy. You can usually market far more effectively in a narrowly focused market.

Earlier, I referred to felt needs versus created needs. Felt needs are those the clients are aware of, such as the need for maintenance, installation, training, and others that are obvious to them. Created needs are needs of which clients are not conscious until a marketer makes them aware, as in the case of computer multimedia applications. The term *created need* is thus not entirely accurate, for the need is not really created; it is felt after the client is educated about something he or she was not aware of before.

Needs, felt & created

Markets for computer consulting vary widely. Clients range in size from individual clients to supercorporations and governments. They offer contracts that vary in size, often unrelated to the size and nature of the client organization. And the markets themselves vary in size, from huge markets— every computer user with commonplace needs—to small, niche markets— those who have special and perhaps exclusive needs. Your initial reaction might be to try to fit all of the large, common market, or perhaps many market segments.

Choosing your markets

Attempting that kind of shotgun marketing—responding to a wide variety of markets or market segments—is a great temptation when one is starting a new practice and eager to capture any possible contracts. However, it is not the soundest basis on which to launch a new practice. It is more sensible to choose a fairly narrow market—a niche or segment of a larger market—suited to your purposes and large enough for you to use as a base.

The term *niche market* means some special segment of the market generally. It is usually characterized by being highly specialized in some way. Perhaps it consists of clients with specialized and perhaps unusual needs, or it requires specialized and unusual skills, or it is a difficult market to reach. It is also relatively small because it is one or more of these things.

A niche market is especially suitable for your purposes for any of several reasons, such as one or more of the following:
- You have outstanding qualifications as an expert in the relevant specialty.
- You happen to have the means to reach prospective clients in this difficult-to-reach market.
- There is little competition for these clients.

There are several pros and cons of addressing niche markets. Usually, the competition for them is limited because they are small markets, and so winning contracts is easier. Often, large organizations think it not worth the effort to pursue the limited amount of business available there. It is usually easier to get firmly established in a narrow specialty and build a reputation there. Time enough later to expand your marketing into additional niches or

Pursuing niche markets

the general market. Your marketing activities are specialized and sharply focused, and so usually produce better results.

On the other hand, because they are small markets, each niche offers a limited amount of business available. It might be necessary to address more than one niche to achieve an adequate marketing base. Occasionally, too, others discover the niche and fight you for business there, so you lose one of the advantages. In most cases, it is to your advantage to start with one or more well-defined niche markets. We'll talk more about this in the next chapter, when we discuss ongoing marketing.

Marketing efforts

For most independent consultants, marketing begins simultaneously with or even before "hanging out the shingle." It involves using personal contacts to recruit a first client, handing out newly printed business cards, mailing announcements, running print advertisements, and otherwise advising the world of your new venture. Essentially, you announce that you are now consulting independently, describe what you offer clients, and solicit their business.

Advertising is usually too expensive for most beginning independent consultants to do on any but the most modest scale, and is too often wasted, for many reasons (discussed in chapter 6). There are, however, a number of other ways to broadcast the benefits of your services at modest costs.

Martin Schiff reports that he won his first contract by posting a notice on the job bulletin board at the University of Central Florida, which he attended. It turned into a client relationship that lasted several years. John Parker used an equally simple and sensible approach to get started. He had a pocketful of business cards he had been given by others in business. He sent each of those individuals his new business card and a brochure. Of the 30 brochures he sent out, he got two responses that he was able to turn into sales. (That is a 0.666 response rate, an excellent return on any mailing!)

Public relations, or *PR*, is an important marketing tool for any new PC consultant. PR means getting free publicity for your venture. Getting publicity is usually far less costly than paid advertising and is often more effective, as well.

News releases

The news release, also called a *press release*, *publicity release*, or simply a *release*, is the basic and most commonly used tool of PR. Figures 4-1 and 4-2 are examples of releases. Figure 4-1 has at least one major shortcoming, however, it has single-spaced text. Normally, news releases should be double-spaced to make it convenient for an editor to mark the copy up for

 **AT&T**

News Release

For further information
Marvin Wamble
214-851-4766

AT&T FIND AMERICA℠ DIRECTORY SERVICE
ENHANCED BATCH APPLICATION
TO BE DEMONSTRATED AT DMA CONFERENCE OCT. 25 TO 29.

FOR IMMEDIATE RELEASE

DALLAS – AT&T will demonstrate here at the 75th annual DMA Conference and Expo on Oct. 25 to 29 the latest feature of AT&T Find America Directory Service – the **Enhanced Batch Application.**

The AT&T Find America Enhanced Batch Application provides a configurable, productivity-boosting solution to businesses that process substantial quantities of directory assistance look-ups.

Enhanced Batch Application offers seamless integration with the customer's systems and operations, allowing efficient, end-to-end batch processing of directory listings.

The AT&T Find America Service is the most comprehensive service of its kind, providing economical access to more than 90 percent of the country's white pages listings. Virtually any business that wants to improve productivity and the accuracy of customer information can benefit from AT&T Find America.

You can see for yourself the Enhanced Batch Application feature and other capabilities of the AT&T Find America Directory Service at our booth – number **2515** – at the Dallas Convention Center, or call, toll-free, **1-800-EBA-1212** for more information.

4-1 *A sample news release.*

publication. It also lacks any indication that the copy ends at the bottom of the page. A reader would be unable to be sure that there is not additional information in pages to follow.

HRH Communications, Inc.

P.O. Box 1731   Wheaton, MD 20915-1731
301 649-2499   Fax 301 649-5745
CompuServe 71640,563

NEWS

November 6, 1992

Contact:
H. Holtz
301 649-2499

For Immediate Release:

USING YOUR PC TO WRITE BETTER PROPOSALS

Herman Holtz, President of HRH Communications, Inc., has announced a new service to aid small business owners win more contracts by improving the efficiency and quality of their proposal-writing activity. In today's economy, all businesses, small and large, must market more aggressively and more efficiently than ever before.

The new service is a one-day training seminar in automating the proposal-writing effort by using personal computers most efficiently in creating and using proposal-writing tools to increase the quality and number of proposals turned out. The coverage will include the adaptation of sophisticated software, such as relational databases and spreadsheet software to handle many of the laborious tasks, as well as building computer libraries of resource materials.

Details of the program are available on request from the company by calling 301 649-2499.

###

4-2 *An alternative style of news release.*

Follow these rules in writing a news release:

- Make it clear that it is a release with such words as *News*, *News Release*, or *Release* appearing prominently at the head of the announcement.
- Be sure that your business name appears plainly somewhere.
- Add the name and telephone number to call for further information.
- Double- or triple-space all copy.
- Print on one side of the page only.
- If the release is more than one page, type *(more)* or *-more-* at the bottom of each page and *###*, *-30-*, or *End* at the bottom of the last page.

You can use a special form or the news release templates supplied with word processing programs such as Ami Pro and Word, but this is not really necessary; you can also use your own letterhead, as in FIG. 4-2.

Both examples shown here included headlines. Although some PR professionals believe that releases should not carry headlines because editors want to write their own, the headline adds a great deal if it summarizes the news in an accurate and attention-getting way. Figure 4-1 falls short of that goal. In fact, I had to read the text before I fully understood the headline. The other headline comes closer to the goal.

Note the line in "For Immediate Release" in both releases. It is customary to use that line, but not absolutely necessary; if it does not appear, the reader will assume that the copy is approved for immediate release. The alternative case is when copy is *embargoed* until some stated date. That would be the case if the release announced a promotion or merger that hadn't been finalized or presented the text of a speech that had not yet been presented, and you wished to have that announcement not made in advance. You might then embargo the release with a line such as "To be released *(date)*" or "Embargoed until *(date)*."

These details aside, the plain and simple idea of a news release is to get some publicity by having it published. The objective must be to make the release newsworthy. Editors do not publish your release to please you, but to please their readers. The editor is well aware, of course, that you seek publicity, but an exchange is involved: you provide the editor with useful material in exchange for getting publicity for yourself.

Newsworthy does not necessarily mean sensational new information, and only rarely presents such information; it means any information suitable for and worthy of being published in that editor's publication. There are, of course, many types of publications. Some are intended for the general population—usually the types of periodicals you find on newsstands. Even they can be subdivided into those intended for almost anyone in the general population, and those intended for people with special interests. Almost anyone might be interested in reading *Time* magazine, for example, but the

Guidelines for releases

market for *Money* or *Popular Science* is somewhat narrower; the market for *Writer's Digest* is still narrower.

There is also an entirely different class of periodicals, known as *trade journals*. Trade journals are directed especially to those in some profession, craft, or industry. For example, I read *Publisher's Weekly*, a trade publication intended nominally for booksellers, but read widely by publishers, who use it to keep in touch with booksellers, and by writers, who read it to keep in touch with the publishing industry.

Understanding this should make it clear why certain items, such as who was hired, who changed employers, who was promoted, which companies merged, and what corporation has reorganized, might be news for a trade journal, but not for a general-interest periodical. Only those working in the industry care to know about these things.

Don't overlook newsletters when compiling your mailing list for your releases. There are many thousands of newsletters, mostly monthly, all specialized in one way or another. Most have limited circulation, a few thousand readers at most. But newsletter readers read carefully, for they pay a relatively large subscription fee for a relatively small package of information each month. You must, of course, keep your release brief when sending it to a newsletter editor, for the newsletter does not afford a great deal of space.

Making your release newsworthy

This is what you must consider when contemplating a news release:

- Who—what readers—are likely to be interested in the information you intend to release?
- What publications reach those readers?
- Which department or editor is right for your item? (Large publications have many departments, and a release addressed to the wrong department or to the publication generally is likely to languish and never reach the right editor.)

Some releases are inherently newsworthy by their subject—a new and different activity, an innovative new product, or significant personnel changes.

If this is your first release and it merely announces the establishment of your consulting practice and the services you offer, that alone might be of interest, especially if the editor who receives your release is having a dull day. But if your release is competing with other items clamoring for publication, your release might not make the cut. Remember that your release is always in competition with other releases and news items.

You might need publicity and not have anything to offer that is obviously newsworthy. In that case, you must take special steps to make your announcements newsworthy. With a little imagination, you can generate many releases worth being published in a number of periodicals.

The key to making your releases newsworthy is to consider the needs and problems of your prospective audience and analyze how your services can be shown to solve those problems or satisfy those needs. Suppose, for example, that you are a PC consultant specializing in training users. It would be possible to generate newsworthy releases by relating computer training to today's economic problems.

Find the newsworthy aspects of what you do or propose to do, just as you tailor the services you offer to the problems of prospective clients. For example, you could adapt the news release in FIG. 4-2 for other circumstances. Instead of proposing to train clients and their staffs in using their computers to automate proposal writing, you could do the same for sales research. The two services would share a common base of instructional modules, with each having one or two specialized modules for proposal writing, catalog development, market research, and sales follow-up.

Consider the following headline of a release:

Many variations are possible

HOW TO USE DATABASES TO IMPROVE YOUR BUSINESS

That headline could be used for a release that promises a number of services:

- Customizing your commercial database software for a better fit to your needs
- Using a database to ensure that you are buying under the most favorable terms
- Help in building customer databases
- Using databases to add direct mail to your sales efforts
- Customizing your databases for tightest inventory control

Similar ideas can be applied to spreadsheets, word processors, and other software, according to the areas and kinds of services you want to provide.

You don't necessarily have to create new programs or add new services on which to base news releases. In many cases, you are doing these things already, but not focusing on the benefit each one provides. Use releases not merely to get your name before prospective clients, but to attract their interest in retaining you to help them solve their business problems. When you get prospects' follow-up calls, you can address their needs and problems more specifically. Any release that appears to offer solutions to readers' problems is almost sure to find a receptive editor waiting.

One rather special type of release, the *product release*, is designed to announce a new product. That information might be of general interest if the product has some special significance that makes it newsworthy, but there are many periodicals, particularly the trade journals, that carry "new product" sections each month. The editors of these departments welcome all product releases because their readers read these sections of the periodical faithfully, always interested in new products.

Reinforcing your releases

Although the release is a well-established marketing tool and every editor knows what it is at a glance, there are ways of improving it further. Some computer consultants follow up their releases aggressively with telephone calls, which does call special attention to the releases and greatly increases the probability that the editor will use it. Some enterprising consultants send at least some of their releases out by fax, another way of getting special attention, which alone increases the probability of publication. In any busy editorial office, dozens of releases arrive daily, and many simply get overlooked by busy editors.

Anything that raises your visibility—makes more people aware of your existence and your services—increases the mathematical probability of winning business. In addition to press releases, there are other ways to raise your visibility and thus improve the odds.

Other PR activities

Public speaking and writing for publication are two other effective ways to gain publicity and raise your visibility. Handled well, these activities can be effective PR in not only elevating your visibility, but in enhancing your professional image.

Speaking

Speaking to an audience lends you a certain prestige, especially if you handle it well and speak with authority and ease. More importantly, it gives you the opportunity to be noticed and remembered by sizable groups of people, rather than individuals. Profitable ways to use public speaking (and overcoming the fear of it) are discussed in detail in chapter 7.

Writing for publication

Unlike speaking, writing does not give you the opportunity to dramatize what you have to say, but it does something else that is just as important. It enables you to reach thousands of people with each presentation (article) you write, making your name and what you do known to many strangers who might otherwise never learn of your useful services.

The advice earlier in this chapter about sending out press releases applies in large part to submitting articles for publication. The most likely targets are the trade journals, both slick magazines and tabloids, and the newsletters. These periodicals are most likely to reach the people you want to address and to publish your offerings. As in the case of public speaking, payment is small or nonexistent, but payment is not the objective here.

Aside from technical articles on subjects related directly to your consulting specialties, you can also write news items—happenings in related industries—and letters to the editor as rather easy means of making yourself known.

One way to ensure publication is to publish your own newsletter. It's a popular marketing device, used quite effectively by independent consultants. However, it takes some time and resources to develop a newsletter, so it might be more appropriate as a promotional device later, when you have gotten yourself established. More is presented on this topic in chapter 7.

Your own newsletter

Sheryl Hergenroeder started PC Insights, Inc. after she'd observed several downsizings in MIS departments. She wanted to ride the trend toward independent consulting, and be able to profit from her own ideas. Hergenroeder set up her consultancy as a subchapter-s corporation to protect her other assets from "errors and omissions" liability. As additional protection, she carefully words the advice she gives, presenting the pros and cons of several options instead of blanket recommendations. In addition to the peace of mind incorporating gives her, Hergenroeder believes a corporation carries more weight than a sole proprietorship among some of her clients.

Profile: Incorporation & marketing

Hergenroeder incorporated for a total cost of about $350, including attorney fees. In retrospect, she believes she could have done it herself with a $25 kit, but only because she had been through the process before in a different corporation. For those considering incorporating, she suggests buying a kit for background information, but using a lawyer to file the papers.

Incorporation

To Hergenroeder, the biggest disadvantage in incorporating is paperwork. She explains, "If I were a sole proprietor, I'd only file estimated taxes and maybe sales tax. Instead, I file 941s, 940s, unemployment, withholding, and personal property tax for both PC Insights and myself." Hergenroeder does the quarterly paperwork herself, although her accountant files PC Insights' year-end returns and provides a mid-year audit of the company.

Hergenroeder currently has about 50 clients, all within a 100-mile radius from her home office in the Maryland countryside. Her first client was her previous employer, with whom she started consulting part-time while still working full-time. She landed the rest of her clients through networking. Hergenroeder recalls, "The first thing I did after starting my own company was to set up lunches with everyone I knew—I paid, of course. We'd have a great time catching up on things, and at the end of the lunch, I'd tell them I was going into the computer consulting business and ask if they could recommend anyone who needed help. I never asked them for work, only for referrals,

Getting clients

although some of them became my clients. I'm still working off that initial marketing effort."

Although she lists several large organizations among her clients, Hergenroeder targets small companies as a source of new business, or, as she puts it, "My clientele is the readers of *Home Office Computing*." Typical clients have included

- An orthodontist with two networked offices who was having problems with memory management and fonts.
- The owner of a hair salon who wanted to track her books on a PC. She needed help not just with the hardware and software, but also with the basics of computerized bookkeeping.
- Two medical secretaries starting their own medical transcription business. They realized they needed a competitive edge, and Hergenroeder supplied it by showing them how to automate some of their work, create a personal letterhead for each doctor they worked for, and customize a medical dictionary.
- An advertising agency on two floors of an office building. One floor had Macs, the other PCs, all hooked together on a network. Hergenroeder was called in to get all the computers sharing resources with each other and with the agency's minicomputer.
- A hospital that needed to download information from a Data General minicomputer to PCs and into Excel spreadsheets.

The hardest part about being a home-based consultant for Hergenroeder is the lack of day-to-day contact with coworkers. As she puts it, "I have no interaction unless I solicit it; I can't just pull people into a conference room to brainstorm with me if I'm stuck." Hergenroeder had to force herself to seek out this interaction, although it made her uncomfortable at first. She makes sure to make at least one marketing call every day, to set up a business lunch or meeting, or just to chat.

Hergenroeder is active in several professional organizations, which has paid off well for her in networking and public relations. For example, as a result of her involvement in an executive women's group, she was interviewed on a local morning news show as a "PC expert." This in itself was great publicity, but she didn't let it end there. Instead, she offered a free, follow-up brochure with tips about buying a PC that viewers could write for. In this way, she not only added to her credibility, but added to her list of prospects.

Hergenroeder feels that it is especially important for consultants working from home to convey a professional image. She advises, "Don't pick up the phone and have the dog barking or the dishwasher running in the background. Get the fax machine, voice mail if you need it, and professionally done business cards and stationery. Everything you do should convey the message that you are a business owner, as well as a technical expert."

5 Advertising & targeted marketing

Many independent computer consultants get new clients principally by referral. At the same time, many computer consultants are unable to rely solely on referrals, and therefore must seek assignments wherever they can find them—from job shops and brokers, by paying commissions to finders, and by advertising. For example, the Monday edition of the *Washington Post* includes a special business section heavy with computer advertising and nearly a full page of classified advertising under the caption "Freelance Connection." There, small businesses, including many computer consultants, make their appeals for work. Among the computer consultants are those advertising programming, hardware and software installations, tutoring, voice/phone/computer integration, desktop publishing, business-plan development, computer-aided design, and other specialties. One calls its service "Rent-a-Nerd" and offers to answer questions and solve problems with charges by the question or by the minute.

It is unlikely that any consultant gets sizable contracts as a direct response to such small advertisements. In fact, many of the advertisers offer free initial consultations, on-site analysis and estimates without obligation, and other such obvious inducements to readers to call, thus becoming good prospects for follow-up as potential clients.

Although businesses do tend to take on lives of their own after a while, winning clients and sales does not usually propagate itself spontaneously in this competitive world. Do everything you can to get repeat business from established clients as the underpinning of your practice, but don't become complacent. Even the largest and most well-established corporations market and advertise constantly to sustain their operations. Witness the most successful supermarket chains taking full-page advertising in the daily newspapers every week, paying for posters on buses and taxicabs, and running many broadcast commercials on radio and TV. There is not a day that they do not offer sales and "specials" to attract business. The time to market is now—today, tomorrow, and every day. Marketing and selling must be permanent activities of your business, carried out routinely and unfailingly.

Advertising principles

Relatively few consultants report any great dependence on advertising for their sales success. Most prospective clients for computer consultants do not turn to advertising to find consultants. They usually demand to know more of the consultant than his or her own advertised claims of excellence, and they do not expect to learn what they want to know in paid advertising. However, understanding the basics of advertising helps you learn to sell. The more you study advertising and selling, the more you discover that their principles are the same, even if their practices vary.

A major problem in all advertising and selling is targeting your prospects. When you advertise in a general medium, such as a magazine or newspaper, you pay for the total audience reached by that medium. That is the basis for the advertising rates charged; it works for all media. But you pay that rate regardless of how many or how few prospects you want to reach.

Print advertising

Suppose, for example, that you advertise in a metropolitan daily newspaper. You pay an advertising rate based on the newspaper's total readership of a million or more readers. The portion of that readership that represents even the roughest and most general of prospects for you, however, is some tiny fraction of that total, perhaps a few hundred or, at most, a few thousand readers. That is not good targeting and certainly not a good investment of your marketing dollars.

On the other hand, if you advertise in a local business journal (assuming that your main targets are businesses), you have greatly improved your targeting. A large percentage of those readers will probably be at least general prospects for your services.

You can go further in your targeting by choosing media that target classes of readers even more closely. If you offer a service that has its greatest application to the legal profession, for example, seek out periodicals that are directed to the legal profession, so that almost all the readers you reach are potential clients. Choose to advertise in the most appropriate of those trade journals discussed in chapter 4.

In practice, you might be able to use the metropolitan daily to do some closer targeting by choosing the location in the publication for your copy—on the sports page, in the business section, or elsewhere in a special section of the paper. In fact, you will probably find different sets of rates for different sections and perhaps even for different days of the week.

Whatever the periodical, the publishers can furnish you with demographic data and *rate cards* (schedules of rates) to help you, and they will usually try to advise you also. It is in their interest to help you get best results and so win more patronage from you.

You might find it useful to do some broadcast advertising on radio and TV. The same principle applies; you pay a rate based on estimated number of listeners or viewers.

Broadcast advertising

Targeting prospects is a bit trickier here, but it can be done. Again, the range of listeners and viewers is quite wide and variable, but identifiable. In general, it is investors and businesspeople who watch and listen to news shows, especially those focusing on business news. It is mostly youngsters who listen to rock music stations. Men in general are the chief audiences for sports programs, especially baseball and football. Talk to the marketers of broadcast commercials to get more information about this. Many of them have well-developed and detailed demographic profiles you can examine.

Again, you will find various rates for various times and spots in the broadcasting schedules, and broadcasters will also furnish rate schedules and counseling.

Most people do not realize that rate schedules are largely fiction or "wish lists." These are rates the publishers and broadcasters would like to charge every advertiser, but rarely are able to, at least with regular advertisers. Advertising rates are negotiable in most circumstances. Experienced, regular advertisers invariably negotiate rate discounts of at least 20 percent and sometimes get discounts of as much as 50 percent of the listed rates. You can usually do as well, once you know that it is possible and are not afraid to ask.

Rate negotiations

Of course, there are exceptions. Occasionally, you run into the stubborn publisher or advertiser who believes it is bad business or harmful to his or her image to give any discount or budge an inch from the rates listed. Still, even they realize that they lose some advertisers that way, and they know that they must offer some inducement to win sales. They can become quite imaginative in the *quid pro quo* deals they invent to close the sales without actually discounting their rates.

Periodical publishers sell space in their publications, and just as any business might have leftover merchandise that has not moved and is costing money to store, a publisher can have leftover space in his or her publication.

Remainders & remnants

Books and periodicals are printed in *signatures* of a certain number of pages. A book can have a few blank pages at the back, where there were not enough pages to fill the final signature, but the periodical cannot be printed with blank pages. It must make the last signature and number of pages for it to come out evenly matched. Filling that unsold space with editorial matter is possible, but it represents lost revenue—cost instead of income. Moreover, the publisher is under a pressure the retailer does not experience: space must be sold before the periodical goes to press, or not sell it at all; waiting for a customer to buy is not a viable option here. Thus, publishers find it expedient to remainder space and sell it as remnants at sale prices.

Publishers do not like to have this widely known, for fear that it will become even more difficult to get listed or even discounted rates for their space, so they have to be pressed to offer remnants of space or to call you when they have remnants available. This is often done in somewhat the same way one "stands by" to take advantage of a last-minute cancellation or no-show on a fully booked flight. In fact, some refer to this as *standby advertising*.

The same thing applies to broadcast commercials, of course. No broadcaster wants to admit it, for the same reasons as publishers, but they have the same problem of unsold commercial time, and a discounted rate for a remnant of air time is certainly better than no income at all from the unsold time.

Other special deals

Experienced mail-order sellers are sometimes able to get a deal from publishers and broadcasters called *help if needed*. In this kind of deal, the publisher or broadcaster guarantees results to a certain extent. They agree to run your advertising or commercial a second time at no charge if the results from the first insertion are disappointing. This is done on trust—the publisher or broadcaster trusts you to report honestly on results, if you want to claim a free second insertion. It is not in your interest to deceive the publisher or broadcaster if the business relationship is to endure.

If you are selling a product—a book, report, or newsletter subscription—you might want to consider the *P.O.* (per order) deal. In this method, you enter into an agreement with the publisher or broadcaster to run your advertising without cost to you, but with a large commission (usually on the order of 50 percent, and sometimes even more) on each order. The order, with payment, comes to the publisher or broadcaster, who deducts the commission and sends you the rest. You then fill the order. Again, publishers and broadcasters do not like it widely known that they enter into such deals, and might flatly deny it if you ask, but it's easy enough to detect the practice. Just watch for publishers and broadcasters advertising products that you must order from them directly, rather than from an advertiser. (In some cases, the publisher or broadcaster uses a post office box as a mail drop, making it somewhat more difficult to detect.)

You might also run into variants and other methods for inducing your patronage. Just remember that you should resist paying the amount on the rate card, at least not without getting some other inducement or tradeoff.

The concept of closer targeting does not stop with selectively choosing media and bargaining for the best deals available. Think of your targets in all your sales and marketing activities, and ponder ways to better improve your targeting.

The marketing database

The objective of databased marketing is to improve targeting of clients to the point of being able to focus presentations on small groups, and even on individuals. Targeting means basing sales appeals on the unique interests of the small group or individual by building a marketing database containing the necessary information about your prospects. Thus, if lawyers, law clerks, and others of the legal profession are your proper prospects, you want to collect such individual data on each one as job title and function, type of law practiced, memberships, interests, age, type of computer equipment used, information needs, public databases subscribed to, and so on.

The original idea for databased marketing was to build an expanding database of detailed information about your clients, using a program such as ACT!, GoldMine, or Maximizer. You keep adding individual information about each client in the database so that the client's profile becomes more and more sharply defined, for marketing purposes, and you can target your clients more and more precisely.

You can then use the database to select a list of clients having one or more characteristics in common that are necessary for your purposes—for example, all clients with offices in their homes and older computers. You can also use the database to identify those characteristics all or most of your clients have in common, then use that information to help you design more closely targeted marketing and sales promotions.

Thus, if you wish to offer a seminar on researching legal information via computer, you can decide who are the best prospects for such a seminar in terms of certain characteristics and interests, and order your database to print out a mailing list of all clients matching that set of characteristics. That ought to win you a high rate of return from your mailing.

Improving the concept

That was the original idea. It seems, in retrospect, much too narrow in several ways. For one thing, why not study the database before deciding what the ideal characteristics are on which to judge the best candidates? With a large enough database, you can do statistical studies and other analyses to guide you in designing the seminar and the mailing package— brochure and salesletter—for greatest effectiveness.

The original idea was also to base the database on one's clients. But why restrict it to clients? Why not expand it to include clients and prospective clients? It is not necessary to mingle clients and prospects in the same database files. If you use a good relational database, as you should, you can keep clients and prospects in separate files, with proper id fields identifying each. Consider, too, that clients are normally defined as those with whom you have done business, those who have bought from you. When you are trying to sell to your clients again, however, they are prospects for whatever you are now trying to sell them. Thus, from a marketing viewpoint, there is no difference between clients and prospects. Everyone to whom you address a sales appeal is a prospect. The sole difference is that you have more information initially about those to whom you have already sold something.

Thus, rather than building a client database, you build a marketing database, consisting of both established clients and prospective new clients to whom you can make offers and solicitations. Or, as a variant, once you have developed one or more profiles of your clients (and perhaps of your best clients), you have a template for evaluating prospects and deciding which ones are most likely to become clients. For our purposes here, then, a marketing database includes both clients and prospects.

Where does the information come from?

The problem in building a good marketing database is getting the information about each individual. In many cases, you start with a few demographic items, but you need more information about personal interests and desires, at least some of which can come only from the individual. In fact, that is how most such databases are built. Individuals are encouraged to provide information via questionnaires, applications submitted to take advantage of rebate offers, free subscriptions, samples, reports, newsletters, or other free items. Frequently, such free items are offered primarily to help gather information for a marketing database.

Putting the database to work

So far, direct-mail marketers and trade publications appear to be the most enthusiastic champions of databased marketing. Of course, it has great application there in developing highly targeted mailing lists and equally highly targeted direct-mail literature.

Don't confine the use of databased marketing to the preparation of advertising and sales literature, however. There is at least one more highly useful application. The information available from a marketing database can be used as an excellent index to the services most appropriate to your business, by indicating what services clients want to buy.

In addition to using databased marketing as a means of marketing your services, it can itself be a special service you provide to others. Many business owners are attracted to the idea of databased marketing, but are not prepared technically to do what is necessary—to build the marketing database. Most small businesses, and even many larger ones, need help choosing the right database programs, designing the fields and formats, and acquiring the knowledge they need to run the systems. This is itself a promising consulting specialty you might wish to consider.

Many pieces of sales literature, like many printed advertisements, display one or more of these faults:

- They make many general statements but few specific ones.
- They make many claims but offer few proofs.
- They have no central theme.
- They make no main point.
- They make too many points.

Take the ordinary brochure, for example. Every brochure ought to have a single, specific objective and a single, central theme. The reader should know from the beginning what he or she is going to learn by reading the brochure.

Don't lose sight of the marketing principles offered in chapter 4. The mere announcement that you now offer LAN services is not going to raise an eyebrow, even among those who know what a local area network is. Unless you are trying to reach other computer professionals to offer your services as a subcontractor, you will be addressing lay businesspeople who don't know why they need a LAN, even if they know what the term means. Your copy must explain the benefit. Here is an example of one way to do that:

Developing targeted literature

Joseph T. Smith
LAN (Local Area Network) Computer Consultant

You don't need an individual modem and printer for every PC in your office. I can save you thousands of dollars by interconnecting your computers so that they share and have access to a single modem and printer. Call or write for details. Free demonstration available on request.

Of course, you can enlarge that to sharpen the appeal, but you can save money by inviting them to call or write for more information. You then follow up with a direct-mail package, usually a sales letter and a brochure. You might also try to get callers to agree to a presentation in their offices, where you will have a better chance to close the sale. Advertising is thus primarily used to generate initial sales leads for follow-up by whatever methods you choose.

One of the key problems in developing an advertising program is that the consultant did not write a business plan before launching the new enterprise, and therefore has not formed a very firm idea of what his or her business is. Often, they do not even know whether they are generalists or specialists within the field of PC consulting, much less whether they ought to represent themselves as generalists or specialists.

The problem with generalists

There is a typical tendency of beginning consultants to be generalists, under the theory that telling the world they can do it all greatly increases the probability of being retained by a new client. Unfortunately, it is a totally false idea.

Computer consultant Michael Schabaschewitz learned that the hard way. He spent a lot of money to turn out very "high class," expensive brochures that made broad but inexact claims and promised to maximize clients' business systems. He was dismayed at the lack of response, but then he had the good fortune to lunch with a savvy management consultant who set him straight: Do it all, if you can, but present yourself as a specialist. The world does not want generalists any more.

Schabaschewitz changed his message to use fear motivation, which was a natural consequence of what he sold—security and disaster recovery methods. He offered prospective clients help in protecting themselves. The results startled him completely. Few of the many clients who began to besiege him actually wanted security measures designed and installed. To his amazement, becoming a specialist made him a much more successful generalist!

He thereupon coined the phrase, "If you want to generalize, specialize." Perhaps that puts too fine a point on it, but it does illustrate what happens when your sales literature makes a single, specific appeal to a single, specific (but common) client problem.

What is your business?

Stop for a moment, and state what business you are in. Computer consulting? Programming? Training? Systems design? Technical writing?

Any such answer may be right, and yet it is all wrong from an advertising viewpoint. It is wrong because it is about you, whereas it ought to be about your clients. One consultant found a remarkable increase in response to his sales material when he decided that his business was not helping people write proposals, but helping people win contracts. Same thing? Not at all, not as a marketing presentation.

Computer consulting, programming, training, systems designing, and technical writing are not what you do; they are how you do what you do. What you do is help your clients achieve their goals, whatever they are— learning how to use a computer, making their programs more effective, speeding up operations, increasing efficiency, or whatever other benefits the client derives as the result of what you do. Providing benefits, the end-results your clients want. That is what clients want to buy, and that is what you must sell.

The role of databased marketing is to help your clients and prospective clients tell you what they want from you. It's easy enough to sell a prospect what he or she wants, but you must first learn what that want is.

One thing to keep in mind in writing any kind of advertising or marketing material is that the material is not about you; it is about the reader, his or her needs and problems, and what you offer to satisfy those needs and solve those problems. Writing effective sales literature requires skill and knowledge of writing and marketing, but it also requires an awareness of the typical problems that trouble clients and compel them to seek help and, of course, technical knowledge of your special field of products and services. Even if you employ a professional copywriter, he or she might furnish the first two skills, but you must furnish the others. I would be alarmed if a copywriter failed to ask me for technical input on who my prospective clients were, why they would seek me out, what I had to sell, and how to express or explain these technical matters in such a way that the reader who did not understand all my technical jargon (used principally to validate my professional status) still got the messages loud and clear.

As David Moskowitz, a Norristown, Pennsylvania computer consultant puts it, his sales literature " . . . is not about me, but rather about my reader's problems and how I can help solve them. I've seen too many brochures that told me more about the writer than I wanted or needed to know. I don't care that the author has a pedigree as long as my arm. I do want to know what they've done that will help me solve my problems."

Advertising and selling both involve making a firm promise to deliver the end-result the prospect most wants, and then proving that you can and will deliver as promised.

Emotion vs. reason

People like to deceive themselves that they make buying decisions based entirely on logic. The truth is that most people are heavily influenced by emotions, if not controlled entirely by them. We tend to rationalize emotional decisions later to salve our consciences. For example, I might persuade myself to spend hundreds of dollars on a 17-inch monitor that I really do not need because everyone else I know is now running such a monitor. I therefore rationalize somehow that I really need this monitor, even though I know that is not strictly true.

Bear in mind that we all act in our own interests as our primary motivation, and that emotion-based desires are usually dominant, even if reason-based desires are battling those emotions (usually a losing battle). Prospects do not buy because they wish to please you or because they accept unquestioningly your assurances of highest quality and other hyperbole. They buy when you convince them that they will gain highly desired benefits by buying. And even then, their motivations are far more likely to be emotional than rational.

For example, suppose you are selling a program to train a prospect's staff in using their computers most efficiently. You might offer several possible arguments:

1. You have great technical qualifications in the subject matter.
2. You have great technical qualifications as an instructor.
3. You have great technical qualifications as a developer and designer of instructional systems.
4. You have a great deal of experience in delivering instruction of this kind.
5. You can present your program on very short notice whenever the client wishes it presented.
6. You will follow up your program with personal monitoring and support of your students' progress in applying immediately what they have learned.
7. You will guarantee an immediate 23 percent improvement in the students' efficiency.

Which of these seven would be most highly motivating to the average prospective client?

The last item, number 7, would probably be the most persuasive. Prospects are usually most motivated by the promise of achieving whatever end-result they most desire. Item 6 would also be highly motivating, although to a somewhat lesser degree because it does not directly promise the desired result. Item 5 is also a desirable benefit.

Were I writing this advertisement, I would stress item 7 and support it directly with item 6. Item 5 would be an additional goodie thrown in to reinforce the sales argument, and the other items would be buried in the body copy to be supportive, but not to compete with the chief item for prominence and appeal. The focus should be sharp and clear on some major item, and should not be diluted with diversionary information that is permitted enough visibility to compete with it.

Tips on writing direct-mail copy

Here are a few reminders to refer to when preparing direct-mail copy:

- Always make things as easy as possible for the customer:
  - ~ Make it easy to understand what you are saying. Use short words, short sentences, short paragraphs. One thought in a sentence, one subject and one main point in a paragraph. (Be sure first that you yourself fully understand the main point.)
  - ~ Make it easy for the customer to order, ask for more information, or otherwise reveal interest by providing a return card, telephone number, or other convenient means for responding.
  - ~ Make it easy for the customer to understand what you want him or her to do by telling the customer what to do. A great many sales are lost by advertisers who fail to tell the customers what they want the customers to do—e.g., "Just fill out the enclosed card." Sounds foolish, but experience proves it to be true.

- A direct-mail cliche (which is nonetheless a truism) is, "The more you tell the more you sell." Don't stint on copy. Be sure to include a letter, a brochure or flyer of some sort, and a response device (an envelope and/or order form) as an absolute minimum, and there is no harm in enclosing even more. Experts claim that three-quarters of the response results from the letter, but that a good circular or brochure can increase response by as much as one-third. My own experience bears this out emphatically. Note how many contest forms require the respondent to remove seals from one place and stick them in another place. This is part of getting prospects directly involved and so arousing their interest.
- Don't tell it all in the letter. Split the copy up among the various enclosures, or at least provide additional details in the various enclosures. Make it clear that additional information and details are found elsewhere in the enclosures. Give the reader good reason to read everything, if you want maximum impact.
- Geography makes a difference. Prospects who are nearby tend to respond better than those at a distance. Know your nearby zip codes, and use them. But do test, for there are always exceptions. For example, when it comes to consulting and speaking services, there is some appeal, even a kind of mystique, to the expert from a distant place, especially if you are mailing from a major industrial or business center, such as New York, Chicago, or Washington. If you are, take advantage of it, somehow, by giving it prominence in your copy.
- If you use envelope copy—advertising and sales messages on the outside of the envelope—do two things:
  ~ Use both sides of the envelope. If you are going to make a bulletin board of the envelope, you might as well get full use of it; copy on both sides pulls better than copy on one side only—if the copy is powerful.
  ~ Now that you've served notice that the envelope contains advertising matter, why pay first-class postage? You might as well save money by using bulk mail or, at least, something less expensive than first class.

In short, decide which end-result the prospect is most likely to want, and stress it as prominently as possible, as a promise. Then structure the rest of your sales arguments to support that promise and prove it logically: Provide the evidence that demonstrates that you can and will deliver on the promise.

6 Selling

No matter how well you do everything else—the technical, managerial, and administrative aspects of your independent consulting practice—you cannot succeed without making sales.

Marketing and selling are not the same thing, although the terms are often used interchangeably. Selling is the final act of marketing—actually getting the order or winning the client.

Marketing vs. selling

Despite the ready availability of good information on sales and advertising techniques, many people believe myths about the subject and ignore the practical truths (if, indeed, they ever encounter them). They often believe that hype—hyperbole—is a sound selling technique. They believe that if they use such superlatives as Madison Avenue has long embraced, prospects will flock to buy. Thus we see a torrent of brochures, radio and TV commercials, and print advertising making loud and unsupported claims of excellence, unconditional guarantees, unparalleled service, and other extreme virtues.

Presumably, the strategy is that the prospect must be finally overwhelmed by all these claimed marvels—the theory that if you say it and repeat it long enough, everyone will come to believe it. Maybe some will, but we are in a society of ever-increasing sophistication, due to modern communication, travel, and record numbers of people getting college educations. Fewer and fewer are naive enough to accept extravagant assertions without question.

Quite the contrary, many people are made even more skeptical by hyperbole, so it backfires quite often.

Consultants often fail because they misjudge what problems prospective clients consider matters of deep concern—what items "strike a nerve" in prospective clients. Being the world's greatest expert in spreadsheets is of little help unless you can back up that claim and a large enough number of your prospective clients want services in that area.

The only sound basis for any sales strategy—planning, advertising, promotion, and closing—is the assumption that clients act out of self-interest and are much more likely to be repelled by, than attracted to, hype.

Creating a business base

Many businesses operate on an ad hoc basis: an entrepreneur finds a single product or idea—a new kitchen gadget or a new way to make money in one's spare time—develops a marketing plan to exploit it, milks the item until interest in it begins to fade, and then abandons it to search for the next idea or product to promote. Computer consulting is not that kind of business. Instead, a computer consultancy usually succeeds when it is built, step by step, on the sound basis of a growing clientele of satisfied clients and a growing set of services that solve the problems of those clients. These must be your objectives to succeed in the long term.

Many computer consultants report that they made their first sales to their former employers. Consultant Hubert Bermont, of Sarasota, Florida, reported that he had difficulty winning a first client because he couldn't cite a reference, such as an earlier client who was happy with his service. He solved that problem eventually by offering to work without charge (as Mark Twain reported he had once done) to show what he could do, and found a client who liked those generous terms, retained him, and even ended up paying him.

Having gotten those first few clients by whatever method, do not get lulled into thinking you can now slow down and do little or no marketing until business becomes slow again. That has been the mistake, and the swan song, of too many inexperienced consultants.

Getting business by referrals

Many independent computer consultants say that they had to market aggressively to win only their initial clients; after that early phase of building a client base, their new business resulted from established clients and referrals. Martin Schiff and John Parker both say that they have not had to advertise for new clients since the early days of building their practices. Bill Rink agrees with this. He says, "I believe that the most important thing you can do is develop a good reputation by providing excellent service at a reasonable price," and agrees that he gets much of his business by referral, but is always alert for other avenues of winning new clients.

Successful PC consultants agree that word-of-mouth advertising—recommendations by their clients to other prospects—is their most effective sales tool. Obviously, you can't hang out your shingle on Monday morning and expect to benefit from word-of-mouth recommendations on Monday afternoon; it takes time for word-of-mouth to build and begin to return results. However, do not sit idly by and wait for it to happen. Most of us cannot afford to wait that long to begin earning income from our consultancies.

Fortunately, there are things you can do to speed up the process of raising your visibility by word of mouth, and even getting referrals and recommendations that way. One well-recommended method of doing this is referred to as *networking*.

Networking is a fairly broad term with many interpretations, even as it applies specifically to sales. In general, networking means making contact with people who can and will recommend you and your services to others or refer specific clients to you. There are several different approaches to networking. You can do it in a fairly passive and informal way, with the word-of-mouth traffic growing spontaneously and with little direct control, or you can use a more direct approach.

The informal approach to networking means pursuing casual ways of creating contacts—acquaintanceships—through participating on electronic bulletin boards, active membership in associations, attending conventions and seminars, and in general putting yourself into situations where you will meet people, many of whom can use your services or recommend you to others who can. Of course, you hand out your business cards and perhaps a small brochure to everyone you meet.

The more direct, organized, and aggressive approach to networking speeds up and intensifies the process of meeting others and making yourself known for what you are and do professionally, as well as what you are as a private individual. This mode of networking involves attending meetings organized solely for networking. All those who attend do so because they have their own networking agendas. (There is usually a fee, used to pay the expenses of the meeting.) Everyone is or should be trying "work the room"; the main objective is to meet everyone present for a brief chat and exchange of cards and brochures, plus giving and receiving leads and referrals. For example, suppose you meet someone who has a new printing business and seeks customers. You might be in a position to give him or her an immediate lead or two. Or, you might meet someone who can give you a lead when he or she learns what you do.

To make the meeting as fruitful as possible, spend only a few minutes with each person. Chat long enough to exchange business cards and perhaps brochures, answer a question or two, and move on. Carry a small notepad to jot notes on, especially when someone has a lead for you.

You might be wondering, "Where do I find such a meeting?" There are two answers to that question. One is to ask everyone you meet during the casual networking you do at association meetings and events what they know about special networking meetings. Eventually you will discover one, and from that you can begin to establish a web of new acquaintances who will invite you to other meetings. (A gentleman named Jerry Rubin, once a noted and notorious "yippy" of the sixties, invited me to one such meeting at the "54 Club" in New York a few years ago. He hosted such a meeting there every week.)

The other way to find a network meeting is to organize your own. It is not as difficult as you might suppose. Arrange a place to hold it, preferably with a cash bar available. (Many restaurants that have a separate, private room will be glad to make arrangements for you, and might not even charge you for the room, relying on the cash bar for their profit.) Ask friends and acquaintances to attend and to invite others to attend. Place a small classified advertisement in the newspaper, if necessary. You will find it easy enough to get such meetings organized, once you have done one or two.

Efficient sales practices

We talked earlier about winning the first few clients. Networking, especially the intensive, highly organized method described, is most suitable as a tool to get started, but is too time-consuming to be a permanent tool or method for selling. This is not to say that you should abandon your memberships and active role in associations and their activities; it is important to maintain such activity at some level, but you must allow yourself enough time to devote to income-earning activity. My suggestion is that once you are established, you should devote not more than one-third of your time to selling and other overhead (non-income-producing) functions. Even within that one-third, shed those functions you can shed. For example, instead of doing your own bookkeeping and filling out tax forms, use an accounting service. Devote as much of that one-third as possible to the far more critical function of winning new business.

The sales tools and practices to design now are the ongoing ones, the ones that will be permanent fixtures of your practice once you have developed them, refined them, and validated their effectiveness. You have seen some of these already, but they are discussed in greater detail now.

Applying databased marketing

Databased marketing is discussed in chapter 5 as a means of asking the prospect to tell you what he or she wants to buy from you—i.e., what you must offer to make the sale. Clever salespeople understand that principle almost instinctively, even if they have never heard the term databased marketing. They approach all prospective clients in a consultant mode, seeking to learn the prospect's wants, needs, and, especially, problems. The salesperson is a consultant too, whose main job is to solve the prospect's problem with whatever he or she has to sell.

Don't approach selling from the viewpoint of how to sell things to your prospects. Approach it as a consultant, someone who needs to learn what the prospect's needs are so you can satisfy them. Do that well enough, and prospects will buy eagerly from you.

Want, *need*, and *problem* are synonymous here. All prospects have problems, want to solve them, and feel a need to do so. Not all are conscious of their problems, however. They might be aware of a few symptoms, but probably have not yet rationalized a conscious need to get help. Even when they do sense a need for help, they often do not know that it is possible to hire someone on a project basis to provide the help or, if they do, how to go about finding someone. In that sense, it is possible to create the need or want.

Getting prospects to tell you how to sell to them—i.e., what their wants, needs, and problems are—is not a simple matter. Even if it were possible to ask prospects directly, you probably would not get the information you want because they are so often conscious only of symptoms or anxieties of some sort, and have not identified the root cause. Still, learning prospects' anxieties furnishes a direct key to identifying and focusing on their needs.

If many of your prospects indicate anxiety about the same thing, you are onto something special. One PC consultant reported trying to help his clients become just a little more self-sufficient in running their computers by giving them a little software program that would teach them such basic functions as copying files between computers and restoring erased files. He was dismayed by how many refused to risk making mistakes even in installing the program—they wanted him to come and do it. It was something he had not anticipated, but there it was, and it indicated to him a need for some effective training program for his clients.

The idea of learning what prospects' problems are as a valuable tool of selling is not new. The notion of a salesperson being a consultant also is not new; it is a widely accepted philosophy of selling that the most effective way to sell is to help prospects solve their problems through what you sell. The idea works in all kinds of selling, whether by mail, by print or broadcast medium, or by personal calls. In fact, it is a broad strategy, but it does depend on getting the necessary information, that *sales intelligence*, by whatever means possible. That sometimes is relatively easy, but sometimes it requires great imagination and resourcefulness, especially when making cold calls.

Selling is itself a consulting function

Cold calling   Personal calls on strangers, usually in person but sometimes over the telephone, are called *cold calls*. When making cold calls, you need to draw the individual out to learn what the problems and needs are. When I made calls on government executives in Washington, I always probed to learn what the anxieties and problems of the individual was, seeking those of greatest concern to the prospect and for which I had remedies to offer.

This approach works very well. Bringing hope by suggesting effective help you can offer makes you a welcome caller. Discovering the problems that are both of major importance to the prospect and can be solved via your services is the most important thing you can do in making sales calls, and should be your first objective.

To get this information, you do not have to rely solely on spontaneous probing, even in calling on strangers. It is possible to do some advance work, in many cases. Actually, if you plan your calls in advance, you can hardly avoid doing at least some intelligence-gathering. There are several ways you can gain a few advance ideas about the prospective client:

- Use the help-wanted advertising to develop a list of prospects. The wording of their advertising itself—the kinds of specialists they need and what qualifications they require—gives you a clue as to their problems.
- Ask around among friends and business acquaintances. You can often gain valuable clues that way. I did over $65,000 worth of business on one occasion as the result of a friend's suggestion about a possible client.
- Send for the prospects' brochures (or find prospects by collecting such literature at conventions and trade shows). These often furnish valuable tips.
- Spend time at conventions, trade shows, exhibits, and other such gatherings getting acquainted with the representatives (i.e., employees) of the various companies, not only of those participating in the show, but also of those attending. Try to do some advance work with these people beyond merely exchanging business cards and chatting. Try to set up calls for the near future. (The calls will then not be "cold," thus overcoming the most distasteful aspect of finding new clients by making personal calls.) As in networking generally, don't lose sight of what you are trying to do: You are working at getting leads for business, and the leads are of little use if you do not create the conditions for a follow-up. If the contact appears to be a promising one, arrange the next step immediately—set a specific date for lunch (never just, "Let's have lunch sometime . . ."), a personal call to meet others in the company or discuss the prospect's needs, or other similar action.
- Monitor contract-award notices as leads to possible subcontracts.
- Apply for inclusion on bidders' lists in government agencies and corporations who contract frequently. In many cases, these prospects request bids and proposals, especially the latter, from all contenders for their business. That makes it important to develop good proposal-writing skills.

Following up cold calls, and even following up meetings and chats with prospects you meet at conventions and trade shows, is a must to close the accounts and win business. Here, too, the proposal is a valuable aid, even if not requested.

The proposal

The written proposal is an excellent means of follow up, certainly among the best next steps you can take. As in the other cases we have been discussing here, to be effective, it must respond directly to a felt need.

The word *proposal* is not entirely a definitive one. Many consultants who say they use proposals are referring to a proposed specification and price quotation. For those who respond to formal *RFPs* (Requests for Proposals), the specification and price quotation are an important part of the proposal, but only a part. A full-blown proposal includes an intense effort to sell the specification proposed at the price quoted.

Should you write proposals?

Some PC consultants decline to write formal proposals. Their reasons are significant. The chief one is cost; writing a full-blown proposal is arduous and expensive. Even for the home PC consultant doing all the work personally, it is costly in time alone. That is not the only cost, however. The process of gathering intelligence to use often involves spending significant amounts of money for consultants, reports, and other necessities. All of this does run up your overhead, of course.

As a gamble, many consultants are convinced, writing proposals is not a good one. In most cases, there are a substantial number of contenders submitting proposals, so that yours is probably one out of anywhere from 10 to 25. The sheer mathematical odds appear to be unfavorable. Still, many consultants write proposals frequently and win often enough to make it worth having done so. (Another reason many consultants tend to avoid writing proposals is because they dislike writing itself, as discussed in chapter 7.

Do not overlook the simple fact that there is a great tendency on the part of many clients to turn to competitive proposals as the chief means for selecting contractors for larger projects. Thus, unless you are willing to write proposals, you are probably limiting your opportunities to win large projects, perhaps even shutting yourself out of some markets.

One other factor to consider: You do not have to have a high average of successful proposals to make the effort worthwhile. You need to win only a small percentage of those you write. All selling costs you time and money, no matter how you do it, and proposal writing is one way to win projects.

Computer consultants who want to work as independent contractors usually must write proposals to win worthwhile contracts. A great proportion of consulting contracts and subcontracts of significant size are awarded only after a proposal competition requested formally by the client. The proposal is the method by which the client judges which applicant is most likely to prove satisfactory and deliver the job at a fair price and when promised. Even if you do not aspire to win and implement substantial projects, proposal writing can be an important sales tool.

The nature of the proposal

Because so many PC consultants are basically engineers and technicians, in the broad sense of the word, they tend to be literal-minded and miss some of the more subtle implications and nuances of the proposal request. They respond to the request with precise answers to all the specific questions of the client, but fail to sell the proposed program. They either neglect to note and appreciate that a proposal is a sales presentation, or they believe that a dispassionate and objective presentation of all pertinent facts—the technical argument—is all that is necessary to persuade a client to award the contract to them. These consultants simply do not understand the most basic principles of sales.

Benefits Facts and logic are not enough to persuade a prospect to buy, of course; a sales presentation needs a great deal more than cold facts to do its job of selling. Advertising and sales executives preach interminably about the need to offer "benefits" and "features," but the client doesn't want to buy "features," and doesn't even think in those terms. The client thinks only in the more primitive terms of "What can you do for me?" Will you save me money? Provide convenience? Ensure reliability—i.e., give me peace of mind? Improve operations? Add to profits? Make my life simpler? Reduce risk or losses?

These are the terms the client finds appealing—the things he or she wants most. Never mind that your proposed program is more efficient; does it produce a direct benefit for the client? If so, be sure to state it and explain it. Don't waste time explaining a feature as your brilliant accomplishment. Promise the benefit and show how the feature provides the benefit—make the promise of the benefit believable.

The whole idea in a proposal or any other sales presentation is to first make the promise—lower taxes, lower operating costs, greater productivity, larger profits, fewer headaches, or whatever blessings you think you can promise—and then prove you can deliver by presenting the technical arguments that, if done well enough, convince the client.

Features Features are among the arguments you make to show how you deliver the promised benefits. If you are pursuing a software manual-writing contract, for example, and want to offer as a feature some special charts that help the reader, don't offer the charts as a marvelous new idea in themselves, but offer them as one of the methods by which your manual will help the reader learn the program much more swiftly, or perhaps not need to really learn the program at all. A feature is only worth mentioning if you can link it to a benefit.

Needs, felt & created   Recall that felt needs are those the prospect is aware of. The prospect who calls and asks you to quote a price for networking four computers in his or her office, or even inquiring as to whether there is some way more than one of the several computers in the office can share the laser printer, is reacting to a felt need. That prospect might not have the foggiest idea of how several computers can use the same printer or the same modem, but he or she does feel a need to find out if it is possible and, if so, what is necessary to do it.

When you are invited to submit a proposal, it is in response to some felt need. The prospect describes the need and asks you to propose a solution and quote a price for your solution. However, prospects are not always conscious of all their needs. You can create a need if you can make the prospect aware of and agree with needs you discover.

If the prospect were to ask you, for example, how he or she could get a special price for three laser printers, rather than one, you might well ask why buy three laser printers. If you then discover that the prospect is completely unaware that he or she does not need a printer for each computer in the office, you might be able to create a need for a LAN by explaining the idea of networking the computers and installing printers and other peripherals as server units. Or, merely by learning that someone you are chatting with has a half-dozen computers in the office, you might inquire whether they are networked, and possibly develop an excellent lead for a LAN installation.

Needs & proposals   Prospects who invite you to submit a competitive proposal do not always have as firm a handle on their needs as they think they do. The RFP includes a statement of work, which supposedly describes the need or problem for which you are to propose a remedy. It might go even further and stipulate the remedy envisioned by the prospect as the right one. Thus the work statement might be wrong or misleading on two counts: the problem might be ill-defined or even incorrect, and the remedy might be poorly conceived or wrong about the current state of the art.

These conditions are not at all unusual. Quite often, a work statement describes the symptoms of the problem instead of defining the problem. That is a common mistake, and an easy one to make for those inexperienced in problem-solving. It is thus not surprising that the prospect's suggested remedy might also be a bad idea. In fact, even when the work statement has identified the problem accurately, the recommended solution might be a bad one. In these cases, a great deal of tact is required in offering a solution that challenges the suggested one, but does not offend the prospect in so doing.

Worry items   Those who write proposals frequently use the term *worry item* to refer to whatever aspects of the procurement appear to be of greatest concern to the prospect. Knowledge of worry items is, of course, highly important. It defines strategies, telling you what to stress most and work hardest at proving.

A worry item might be cost, or concern over the ability of the proposer to meet a difficult schedule, or feasibility of the solution, or several other things. Sometimes it is easy to identify such items because the work statement stresses their importance. In many other cases, however, it is far from easy to determine which elements of the project (and, thus, of the proposal) are the most critical. Whether deliberately or otherwise, many work statements give few clues to identifying the most critical items. This is true even with government RFPs, for which regulations mandate that some objective rating scheme be used and explained to the proposers.

Proposal format

The proposal format I use and recommend is designed to achieve the following objectives:

1. Introduce yourself as an interested and qualified contender for the project.
2. Demonstrate your complete understanding of the client's problem, need, or want.
3. Present your approach, with analysis of the client's need and explanation of why your proposed approach is the right one. (You might have to educate the client in doing this.)
4. Present your plan, implementing what you have said before, making your commitment to specific activities, schedules, and deliveries.
5. Support all of this with a presentation of your qualifications to carry out the plan and evidence of your dependability as a contractor.

In a formal proposal, the standard format I recommend has four chapters or sections. You will find a general four-part proposal outline adaptable to most proposals. (Even when clients mandate a proposal format, they generally do not differ greatly from this.) There are cases, of course, where a special format should be used. For example, where your study of the RFP suggests that some aspect is of special importance to the client and you have a great deal you want to say about it—project management, for example—consider the wisdom of stressing that by treating the subject in a separate chapter or section.

On the other hand, where you are pursuing a small job that does not require or justify a full-blown, formal proposal, you will want to prepare an informal proposal, often referred to as a "letter proposal." This will probably be not more than three to five pages, written as a letter. However, that does not change any of the truths of sales, nor make the proposal less of a sales presentation. A letter proposal must do the same job the formal proposal does, even if on a smaller scale, and it must present the same kind of information.

Nothing is more important to the marketing of your professional services than the proposal, used properly and with a few tips in mind:

- Analyze the client's problem closely and be sure that you understand it fully before committing yourself to a plan of action. Don't rush to the word processor before you have done so.
- Devise a specific strategy upon which to base your proposal.
- Be highly specific in what you propose to do and furnish to the client.
- Shun hyperbole. Stick with nouns and verbs, using adjectives and adverbs as sparingly as possible. Especially avoid superlatives.
- Quantify as much as possible when providing details.
- Avoid potential disputes by being sure to specify exactly what your quoted cost estimate covers.

Graphics—drawings, charts, and graphs—add greatly to clear and easy communication of ideas. By all means, use them in your proposals. With today's computers and software, anyone can prepare professional-quality graphics.

A good illustration requires little explanation, and that is the way to test the quality of any illustration. Is the illustration clear or is it "clever"? Forget about clever devices and artistic considerations; the purpose of an illustration is to communicate information accurately and efficiently. If the reader has to puzzle over the meaning or study the illustration to understand it, he or she will probably set your proposal aside with a sigh, and go on to the next one. Make it as easy as possible on the reader. Cleverness is all too often the death of meaning and understanding, and therefore the death of the sale.

For function charts, use the *Why? How?* technique to generate the chart and to test it. Going from left to right (or from top to bottom, if you prefer that progression), ask "Why?" of each box, and the answer should be in the next box. Going the other way—in reverse—ask "How?," and the answer should be in the next box. If the answers are not very clear, consider adding boxes (for more detail) or changing the wording in the boxes. (Charts, like text, should go through drafts, editing, reviews, and revisions.)

Using headlines, glosses, & blurbs

Proposals are not exciting literature, and at best are fatiguing to read in quantities, as prospects are compelled to do. Anything you can do to make it easier for the reader will help you, in more than one way: it helps you get your own messages across and pierce the consciousness of readers who might be reading mechanically and without full appreciation by the time they get to your opus; and you earn the reader's gratitude, which can do nothing but help your case. There are at least three devices that add interest to text:

Headlines Use headlines as freely and as often as you can. Use them to summarize messages and telegraph what a paragraph or page is about. But use them also to *sell*. That is, use the headline to summarize promises—

benefits—and proofs. Use them to remind the reader of the benefits and reinforce the proofs.

Glosses   A *gloss* is a little abstract in the margin of a page that summarizes the text next to it. Usually, there is at least one gloss on a page, and often there are several. Like headlines, glosses can and should be used to help sell the proposal by focusing on benefits and proofs.

Blurbs   A blurb is very much like a gloss, except that it is not used as frequently, and is thus somewhat broader in scope and, usually, of greater length. A blurb generally appears after a major headline or chapter title. Like headlines and glosses, blurbs should be used to sell, as well as to sum up information and break up large amounts of text.

A proposal outline

A proposal outline with four parts, plus front matter and back matter, is provided here. This format may, of course, be modified to suit your own preferences, the circumstances, or the dictates of the client. (An informal or letter proposal would not have front and back matter, nor separate chapters, although it would follow the general philosophy of this outline.) Some RFPs mandate a proposal format, and some companies have a standard format specified for their proposal, either of which you would of course follow, in such a case.

1. Front Matter
   - Copy of Letter of Transmittal
   - Executive Summary: Abstract of the most important points that demonstrate your best arguments.
   - Table of Contents

2. Section or Chapter I: Introduction
   - About the Offeror: Briefly introduce your firm, sketch your company and qualifications, refer to details to be found later, and make other opening statements.
   - Understanding of the Requirement: Make a brief statement of your understanding of the requirement, in your own language (don't echo the RFP). Leave out the trivia and focus on the essence of the requirement, providing a bridge (transition) to the next chapter.

3. Section or Chapter II: Discussion
   Discuss the requirement, analyzing, identifying problems, exploring and reviewing approaches (with pros and cons of each). Include similar discussions of all relevant matters—technical, management, scheduling, and other important points, including worry items. This is the key section in which to sell the proposed program, make the emotional appeals (promises), explain the superiority of the proposed program, and demonstrate the validity of the proposer's grasp of the problem, how to solve it, and how to organize the resources. This section should culminate in a clear explanation of the approach selected, bridging directly into the

next chapter. Include graphics, as necessary, especially a functional flowchart, explaining the approach and technical or program design strategy employed.

4. Section or Chapter III: Proposed Project
This is where the specifics appear—staffing, organization (with an organizational chart), and resumés. Key elements are these:
- Project management: Procedures, philosophy, methods, controls; relationship to parent organization, reporting order; other information on both technical and general/administrative management of the project. (May be separate chapter or even separate volume, for large projects.)
- Labor-loading: Explain major tasks and estimated hours for each principal in each task (use tabular presentation), with totals of hours for each task and totals of hours for each principal staff member.
- Deliverable items: Specify, describe, and quantify.
- Schedules: Specify using a milestone chart, if possible.
- Resumés of key staff: Probably just you, but possibly associates or other consultants.

5. Section or Chapter IV: Company Qualifications
Describe company, past projects (especially those similar to the one under discussion), resources, history, organization, testimonial letters, special awards, and other pertinent facts.

6. Appendices (Back Matter)
Append detailed data, drawings, papers, bibliography, citations, and other material that some, but not all, readers will want.

Proposal-writing capability

The hardest proposal to write is your first one. The worst thing that can happen to you is to have that first one win the contract. As in the equally unfortunate case of winning the first client you approach, the experience gives you a false sense of what is required. It's easy, in those circumstances, to believe that winning contracts and clients is ridiculously easy or that you have a natural capability for selling. Such fortune is usually followed by a series of efforts that are not as successful, and that can easily lead to despair.

The first proposal you write probably won't win anything but a thank-you from the client and an invitation to try again. The only people who win all or nearly all the contracts for which they write proposals are those who are extraordinarily selective and pursue only what they deem to be sure things. Most of us come to accept that we won't win them all, but we must win often enough so that our overhead can tolerate the expense.

Proposal strategies

Strategies make the difference in proposal writing as in many other things. Proposal skill is not entirely writing skill, important though writing skill is. It is also selling skill, imagination, practical application, and attention to detail. One strategy, mentioned earlier, is to concentrate on worry items. But there are other strategies.

Innovations—fresh, new ideas—are the basis for many successful strategies. In winning a contract to train postal personnel in maintenance of a new bulk-mail processing system, I put innovation to work. I made a case for the difficulty of properly weighting the course—creating a perfectly legitimate worry item. I then gave the client a solution, which I had invented: a failure probability analysis.

Some famous inventors and engineers have maintained that there is no such thing as a really new idea. They say that a so-called new idea is merely a new arrangement of old ideas. The failure probability analysis was a good example of that thesis. It was the well-established reliability analysis turned around to be more useful for designing a maintenance program.

Innovation vs. imitation

John D. Rockefeller allegedly believed in imitation. He was reported to have advised that success is observing what some other successful person is doing and doing the same, only better. It is not bad advice, and it certainly worked for him, but doing something better is itself innovation!

Innovation works well in proposal writing, if it can be shown to produce improved results—benefits to the user. Show a client how a PC set up in his or her home can be used to work with a computer miles away in an office and you get attention. Show how that delivers a benefit—saves money, enables the client to work at home and find that work ready and waiting on the office computer the next morning, or other windfall—and you are well on your way to a sale.

You do not have to invent the lightbulb or find the Rosetta Stone to be innovative. In fact, the last thing you want is an innovation that is truly revolutionary, for then it strains the imagination and is difficult to sell. Most of our progress is not revolution, but evolution: gradual change and improvement.

The cost of proposal writing

Proposal writing is expensive. Many consultants are sure that they can't afford it. The fact is, proposal writing is most expensive in the beginning. It should become much easier—and therefore cheaper—with experience.

However, do not rely on experience alone to bring down proposal-writing costs; there are other ways to cut those costs. You should pursue all of these. Remember that this is based on the premise of commitment to proposal writing as an ongoing sales effort. It is not necessarily something you do every day, but you should do it on a continuing basis by making sure that you are aware of every proposal-writing opportunity that is likely to be of interest to you, and that you study and evaluate each opportunity, responding when your evaluation tells you you should do so.

You must begin building a *proposal capability*, which is a set of resources that cuts proposals costs in two ways, by reducing your direct costs for writing a proposal, and by increasing your win ratio.

The proposal library   One of the resources that cuts proposal-writing costs significantly is a proposal library consisting of file copies of all your own proposals, any competitive ones that fall into your hands (some will, from time to time), and any other literature of competitors. Save everything.

Read and shelve books, brochures, articles, and everything else you can use as reference materials, both about proposal writing and about the subjects you cover in your proposals.

Read the trade magazines that cover your markets. Keep abreast of what is happening, where it is happening, and to whom it is happening. Clip pertinent materials and file them.

Swipe files   Build proposal *swipe files*, including your own older proposals—on disk, of course—and anything else that you can legally use by simply embodying it in one of your proposals or rewriting it according to your needs. Many of the resources in your proposal library can become swipe files.

Boilerplate   Certain elements of your proposals will remain much the same in each case, or will require only updating and minor change each time. Descriptions of your past projects, general experience, physical facilities, and similar information can become *boilerplate* that you occasionally polish, but remains essentially unchanged. This is a valuable resource in cutting proposal costs.

Capability brochures & bidders lists

As a PC consultant, you should have a *capability brochure* (also referred to as a *capability statement*). This is not the handy, pocket-sized leaflet that describes your venture in 500 words and invites the reader to call or write. Rather, it is a second cousin to the proposal, and is useful for all consultants, but especially for those who want to be included on a maximum number of bidders lists.

Most organizations who use consultants and contractors regularly have one or more bidders lists for the specialties in which they normally require services. There might be a bidders list for programmers, another for technical writers, another for systems engineers, and so forth.

Occasionally, a government agency or some other organization will be planning a procurement of services for some highly specialized need, for which they do not have a bidders list or have bidders lists they think are out of date. The organization then posts a notice wherever they post notices inviting bids and proposals (in the *Commerce Business Daily*, in the case of federal agencies), describing the impending procurement briefly and inviting those interested in being placed on the bidders list to submit a capabilities statement. Those whose statement is acceptable will be placed on the bidders list, and will eventually receive an invitation to bid or propose (usually these procurements call for proposals).

Such a capability statement or brochure follows the same logic described for a proposal, but discusses and describes your capabilities generally for the type of work you do, the problems you solve, and the needs you satisfy. You describe your experience, past projects, facilities, resources, and whatever else is pertinent to identifying the capabilities and services you offer.

It's a good sales practice to have a standard capability statement or brochure to send out and leave with people. Should you run into a special request, and your brochure does not match the request closely enough, you can modify and customize it to suit. Update your brochure, too, as you complete new projects and acquire new resources that ought to be added to your statement.

For these reasons, you don't want to have a large quantity of such brochures. They do not have to be expensive brochures in color; far better that they be easy to update. Thus, it is probably a better idea to create your capability brochure on your PC, where it can be maintained and printed out as needed. You can have an attractive cover or binder in which to enclose it, but you do not need to go to great expense to create the information to go between the covers.

Prepare a standardized letter to go with your brochure, customized to make it clear that you wish to be invited to bid or propose on all requirements, and pledging that you will respond.

Pursuing government contracts

Individuals can do business with federal agencies, just as major corporations do. (I have personally won and performed on many government contracts.) The advantages of doing business with the government far outweigh the drawbacks. The following suggestions will help you get started learning the ropes of selling your services to the government.

To get on bidders lists, ask for Standard Form 129, "Application for Bidders List," and make enough copies to distribute to the various agencies with whom you think you can do business.

To learn of outstanding bid and proposal opportunities, subscribe to the *Commerce Business Daily* (CBD) or to any public database that carries CBD Online, such as CompuServe. Also, visit government bid rooms and monitor the notices on the bulletin boards. Don't depend entirely on Form 129.

If you are near a General Services Administration Business Service Center, take the time to visit and talk to the people there. They are located in Boston, New York, Philadelphia, Washington, Atlanta, Chicago, Kansas City, Denver, Houston, Fort Worth, Los Angeles, San Francisco, and Seattle. If you are not near one, write to the one in Denver:

Denver Federal Center
Building 41
Denver, CO 80225

and request all available information on doing business with the government. Write to the contracting offices of major agencies—the Department of Defense, NASA, Health and Human Services, and others—and make the same request for information.

Watch the CBD for announcements of free seminars on competing for federal contracts. They are held frequently, sponsored by members of Congress in their districts.

Get acquainted with the contracting officers of federal agencies near you. Personal contact helps a great deal in all marketing, and a friendly contracting officer can be very helpful.

7 Writing, speaking, & profit centers

Counseling others and doing for them what they can't or don't want to do for themselves is a field with more income opportunities than you might realize.

Professional speaking and writing complement consulting nicely. Many public speakers also consult and write, many writers also speak and consult, and many consultants also speak and write.

Writing and public speaking abilities are valuable assets in consulting, as in business generally. They can make a great difference in the degree of success you achieve in consulting and in building your practice. In fact, these abilities are more than assets; they are necessities. You need them to market successfully, to communicate well with others, and to deliver your services successfully. It is possible to minimize the amount of writing or speaking you do, either by avoiding situations that call for them or by having others do them for you. However, you will thus forego some important benefits and incur more expenses.

Writing & speaking are important

Fortunately, writing and speaking support each other; mastering one strengthens your ability to do the other. It is not a coincidence that many professional speakers are also writers and consultants. Consultants must communicate. Several of the computer consultants who report that they get virtually all their new business by referrals agree that their ability to communicate well with their clients is key to winning client loyalty and getting referrals.

I asked Martin Schiff what he thought to be his most important asset, aside from his technical skills. He replied immediately that it was his ability to communicate well with his clients. That is what gains their confidence in him and leads to repeat business and referrals, he said. Bill Rink, of whom I asked the same question, also considers communication a key element of success. He points out that clients don't want to learn the technical jargon he works with; they appreciate getting explanations in language they can understand.

That is one side of the benefits package. The other side is that writing and speaking are keys to adding income centers to your consulting practice. This diversifies your business base, adding stability and increased ability to weather economic peaks and valleys.

Much of what follows is intended to enhance your marketing, but in many cases you can also use what you learn here to produce income—substantial income—to supplement your basic consulting income. In fact, sometimes the additional income-producers begin to overshadow and outproduce consulting services themselves!

The art of writing

You might never learn to enjoy the act of writing, as I do, but you can learn to do it in such a way that it is not a painful or unpleasant duty. It is not my intention to teach you how to write, even if I thought I could do that; that would be far beyond the scope of this book. I proceed from the reasonable premise that your writing skills are at least average and already adequate to most of the writing needs you will encounter as a computer consultant. My intention is to help you learn how to take most of the pain out of writing and use it to further your success as a computer consultant.

It is certainly no secret that many people, even executives and professionals, shrink from writing and avoid it as much as possible. Colleges have long taken note of this and installed mandatory writing courses, especially in the sciences and engineering curricula. Government and private employers are also aware of the problem and consider it important enough to offer business writing courses to employees. Such courses have even been made mandatory, such as when the federal government set up a staff to rewrite federal procurement regulations a few years ago.

Whether individuals resist writing out of distaste for the act of writing, as so many claim, or out of fear of what they deem a formidable task, it is certainly a fact that they do resist doing it. It probably explains why so many of the letters you and I write go unanswered. Even my letters to suppliers requesting something are often either unanswered or answered only after a lengthy delay and perhaps a second, follow-up letter. This reluctance to write extends even to writing simple business correspondence. It accounts also, at least in part, for the reluctance of many to write proposals, thus foregoing an important source of clients.

Because of this and despite my preference for writing as a means of communicating with others, I sometimes compel myself to use the telephone, rather than the mails or even the fax, when I need a prompt response. There is no doubt that the telephone is the most direct and fastest means for conveying information. It is also a superior means of communication when a spontaneous exchange of information is needed and time is a major consideration. The professed need for instantaneous communication is often a false one, however. Rather, many people find the telephone a more convenient means of communicating with others, even if it is not always the best means.

Each means of communication—written and verbal—has advantages and disadvantages, but writing is important to the home-based computer consultant in a number of ways:

The advantages of writing

- You cannot be interrupted before you are finished; you are able to say it all, every sentence, word, and syllable, at your own pace and until you are finished.
- You can plan carefully, at your convenience, everything you want to say and the order in which you want to say it, polishing your words until you are thoroughly satisfied with your presentation.
- You are not at the mercy of the reader's alertness or ability to grasp immediately everything you utter, as you are in making oral presentations. Reading a written presentation, the reader can absorb the information at his or her own preferred pace, read again what you have written, and even study it, if necessary, to be sure he or she has it all.
- When you have written something persuasive in making a sale, your reader can pass your material around to others who might be involved in making purchasing decisions. (Or you can furnish several copies of your presentation so everyone can read at his or her convenience.) Writing ensures that you have made the same presentation to everyone. Otherwise, you are at the mercy of the individual's ability to present your thoughts to others accurately.
- After the initial time spent developing a piece, you can use it over and over with very little time or expense required.
- As a home-based consultant, you might not have the equipment or resources to handle large volumes of business over the fax or phone.
- There is, finally, one great advantage that derives from the reluctance of so many others to write: You gain an advantage over many of your competitors, those who pass up proposals and other sales opportunities because they resist writing.

For all of these reasons, both you and your clients enjoy a number of special benefits when you offer written presentations to them. Writing is not as difficult as some imagine; almost everyone with an average fluency in our language can probably already write acceptably well or can certainly learn to do so.

Writing tips

Much of the difficulty in writing revolves around two factors: uncertainty as to format and grammar, and lack of planning.

You can't build a proper house, prepare a proper dinner, or conceive a great symphony without a plan; nor can you write a proper proposal, brochure, newsletter, or anything else without some planning. Planning means gathering up the information you need, setting a specific objective, and outlining the presentation. The preparation of the outline is by far the most difficult part of the job, in most cases. It is the task wherein you must analyze the material or information you have and organize it to meet the objective you have set. In most cases, that objective will be to inform, report, educate, argue, persuade, defend, or sell. (For an ordinary letter, the planning and outlining might be all in your head, but the principle is the same.)

Decide first just what the other party wants or ought to get—an answer to a question, a response to a complaint, a price quotation, a persuasive argument, an explanation, an apology, or whatever else. Decide how you ought to respond. If you have been asked a question, should you make a straight and unequivocal answer to the question, a qualified answer, a request for more information, or some other response? Don't be too hasty here, responding by reflex without thinking through the consequences of an unreasoned response. You must be absolutely certain that you fully understand the wants of the reader you are addressing, and you must think out carefully what your proper answer or appeal ought to be.

Technical writing

Many computer consultants are attracted to the technical writing field because there is an apparent need for better documentation. Hardware documentation is not better than the existing software documentation, but there is a much greater demand for documenting software systems, so the greater opportunity for technical writing is in the area of software manuals.

The need is for simplicity. The average user is already a bit apprehensive about coping with the mysteries of the computer. He or she is fearful of doing the wrong thing, despite all the assurances that pushing the wrong keys will do no harm, even if it crashes the program. Here are a few keys to such writing:

- Run the program through all its paces to be sure that you thoroughly understand it.
- Read all the help files and pull-down menus. It will probably be a great help to print them out and use them for reference as you write.
- Organize all explanations logically—i.e., in the probable order in which users use and learn the program. Review your organization plan until you are satisfied that it is a logical progression.
- Study everything you write for ambiguity: Can it be misunderstood or misinterpreted? If so, revise it to eliminate that possibility.

- Will drawings help? If so, make sure they are self-explanatory. A drawing that requires a lot of text to explain it is a poor illustration.
- If you must use jargon, add a glossary to explain all special terms.

Newsletters

The newsletter can be a great marketing tool for independent computer consultants, quite possibly the best one. I have found it highly productive in supporting my marketing efforts for a variety of reasons, including at least these:

- It gives you great credibility, affording you a medium for friendly "conversation" with clients and prospective clients.
- It builds your image as a highly respectable professional.
- It affords you an avenue to other publications, serving as an effective public relations effort.

Another attractive aspect of newsletter publishing is that it is one of the few businesses in which you get the money up front because subscriptions are usually paid a year in advance. That alone does your cash flow some good.

Newsletter publishing has its problems, of course, chief of which is the always impending deadline, the date the next issue must go to press. It is always astonishing how swiftly the time goes between deadlines, especially if you publish on the most popular schedule, monthly. The way to minimize this problem is to publish bimonthly or even quarterly, at least in the beginning. You can always increase the frequency of your schedule later, if you wish, but the reverse is not true: It is not easy to go from monthly to bimonthly.

Using the same reasoning, it is best to start with four pages. Again, you can add pages later, if necessary. That keeps your printing costs down and also reduces the burden of gathering enough good material for each issue. Once you gain some experience, however, you will probably find yourself with an abundance of material for each issue. Newsletter editing should follow the principles of good journalism, far too many to be listed here, but there are many articles and books on the subject readily available.

Newsletter formats

The very idea of being a publisher, even of such a modest publishing effort as a newsletter, intimidates many beginning consultants. It need not. Publishing can exist at all levels.

Some of the most successful newsletters of the pre-PC era were published in modest formats, typed on manual typewriters on 8½-×-11-inch paper. Two of the most famous and most successful of that genre are *The Kiplinger Letter* and *The Gallagher Report*. Austin Kiplinger was quite frankly trying to launch a for-profit business, and succeeded quite beyond his most ambitious hopes. Bernard Gallagher was a different case, one more appropriate to this discussion. He sold securities to individual investors, and he started his newsletter as a freebie, hoping to stimulate sales and win new clients. In a short while he discovered a startling fact: Investors found the information in his newsletter valuable and wanted to pay to ensure that they would continue to get it! Soon enough, Gallagher made publishing that newsletter his chief business.

Even when electric typewriters arrived in offices everywhere, with their carbon ribbons and superior output, Gallagher continued to compose his newsletter by manual typewriter, as did many others. There was a certain mystique to the ugly and crude copy produced by old Underwood and Remington manual typewriters. It connoted up-to-date, last-minute freshness of information. Image is always important in marketing, and it is as important in a newsletter as it is in other arenas. It is difficult to get this idea across to some people, but too polished an appearance in a newsletter can be self-defeating.

A great deal of effort has been put into the development of desktop publishing programs, with major emphasis on their ability to produce attractive newsletter formats with the PC. Many aspiring newsletter publishers of today take all of this quite seriously, and often devote an enormous and quite disproportionate share of their time and effort to the pursuit of the "right" software and newsletter formats. They tend to become preoccupied with the cosmetic side of newsletter publishing, rather than with the editorial side.

This is unfortunate if you want to publish a newsletter for the practical benefits it can bring to your business. The fact is that the reader does not attach any great importance to the physical appearance of the newsletter beyond the obvious difference between the amateurish and the professional presentation. Figure 7-1 is one example of a simple newsletter composed with a popular word processor and printed on a laser printer. It is entirely adequate for most purposes.

You can spend a great deal of time and money to make a more artistic newsletter, with many sophisticated physical features, but they will not add significantly to the newsletter's value or effectiveness. In fact, greater artistry might have a negative effect by distracting the reader from the essence of the newsletter: its content and timeliness. The more polished the image becomes, with multicolor printing and sophisticated typography, the less timely the information appears to be. An overly slick and professional appearance appears to be "hype," and is therefore self-defeating.

You can charge a subscription fee for your newsletter, or you can make it a free one. Should you publish a free newsletter for your clients and prospects, never think of it as a free item and never advertise it as free. Post a substantial

WRITING FOR MONEY

"No man but a blockhead ever wrote except for money."

--Samuel Johnson, 1776

Special Edition	Editor/Publisher Herman Holtz	$60/year
	P.O. Box 1731 ■ Wheaton, MD 20915	

Nothing in the world can take the place of persistence. Talent will not; nothing is more common than unsuccessful men with talent. Genius will not; unrewarded genius is almost a proverb. Education will not; the world is full of educated derelicts. Persistence and determination alone are omnipotent.

--Calvin Coolidge

DREAMERS AND DOERS

There are those who only dream of being successful and those who do something about it, something to make themselves successful. Which you are depends on you. No one can make you a success, and no one can prevent you from becoming one--except you.

My goal was to become a successful freelance writer, and I did--50 books and hundreds of articles, essays, and other pieces published with my byline. It took me a lot of years to do it. I started late through circumstances I could not control: the Great Depression of the thirties and World War II, which occupied five years of my time. But I didn't let obstacles and delays discourage me. People who get discouraged do not succeed, and I always knew that it is never too late to start. (I wrote almost all my books after I was 60.) The time to start is always *NOW*.

ANYONE CAN BE A SUCCESSFUL WRITER

I want to help you make that start right now. I have a list of special monographs-- reports-- that will guide you. I feature reports on writing and how to succeed at it--not how to write, but how to sell what you write--how to *succeed* as a writer. It takes a certain kind of talent to be a Mark Twain or an Ernest Hemingway, but anyone can be a successful writer of more modest achievements. The world is full of highly successful writers

Copyright 1992 by Herman Holtz

whose names you never heard. They write brochures, memos, catalogs, reports, and sales letters, among other things. My reports tell you about these--what you can write, who wants your help, and who is willing to pay for it. I show you what to write and how to sell it. But not all my reports are about writing. Many are about other subjects--e.g., marketing, grants, loans, and consulting.

Writing for Money (WFM)--this newsletter-- will appear each month as a compendium of information and guidance for independent writers, experienced veterans, struggling newcomers, and hopeful beginners. It will cover a variety of material, including tips on markets, ideas, and knowhow.

A VERY SPECIAL FEATURE

As a unique service, I will respond directly to you, if you are a subscriber, answering your questions and advising you to the best of my ability. That is a bonus for subscribing.

FREELANCING OPPORTUNITIES GREATER THAN EVER TODAY

WFM offers tips, ideas, and guidance for freelance, independent writers. It is geared to the modern technology that writers use today --computers with word processing, spell checkers, desktop publishing, etc. It will also cover fax machines, modems, copiers, and other tools that give the writer of today a power and capability as never before. The following are just a few of the kinds of information you will normally get:

1

7-1 *The first page of a simple newsletter.*

price on it, and arrange for your clients and prospects to get complimentary subscriptions. Make them do something positive, but easy, to get complimentary subscriptions, such as making a formal request on their letterhead or filling out a brief questionnaire. This not only demonstrates that you do value the newsletter and don't use it as a throwaway circular, but it also provides information for your marketing database.

Getting material

Many consultants are reluctant to start a newsletter because they fear they will not have an ample supply of news items to use. In fact, that proves to be the smallest problem. It is more of a problem to glean the best and most useful items from a surfeit of data. For one thing, as soon as others become aware of your newsletter, you will get their news releases. You can accelerate this process by requesting your name be added to distribution lists.

Combinations of words can be copyrighted; information cannot. You are free to report on information you gain from other publications, if you write it up in your own words. You can use news releases by quoting them verbatim, if you choose. They are sent to you with the hope that you will quote them directly, preferably *in toto*.

Invite contributions from others. Many people are delighted to write for publication. Give them recognition—bylines for their contributions—to encourage them. Exchange complimentary subscriptions with other newsletter publishers with mutual permission to quote from each other's publications.

Your newsletter is usually limited in space, so be sparing with language. Write succinctly, but with the expectation of editing your draft and boiling it down. In general, good editing consists of boiling down the drafts. Even the most accomplished professional writers tend to overwrite, but unless you are some rare genius, you cannot do nearly as good a job of judging what to keep and what to eliminate when writing your drafts as you can afterwards, when editing them. Therefore, write it all, in all its details. Then decide what is important and what is not.

Writing for publication

Writing is an activity of many consultants, and it offers you an opportunity, if you wish to take advantage of it. All those PC periodicals represent a market for you; few of them are written entirely by staff writers. Almost all the material is contributed by individuals who are paid for their articles. Computers, however, are a subject of interest to so many people that you need not confine yourself to writing for the low-paying trade and technical markets. You can write for many of the more popular periodicals, usually for quite substantial fees for your articles. These include such a wide variety of magazines as *Inc.*, *Popular Mechanics*, *Popular Science*, *Money*, *Home Office Computing*, *Entrepreneur*, and many others.

Approach this type of publication by studying it to get a sense of its style and the kinds of materials it runs. But don't write your article yet. Periodicals rarely use unsolicited manuscripts. They want a query letter that briefly proposes, in a page or two, your article. Include an outline, and estimate the length of the article. Send that to the editor and wait. Some writers believe in waiting two or three weeks and then calling the editor to follow up, and it seems to work for them, but some editors prefer that you wait for them to call you. If the editor is interested, he or she will call to talk to you and probably make an offer. If not, there are other periodicals at which to try your luck.

Writing books

The computer book market is a huge one. Visit any large bookstore and spend a little time browsing the shelves of computer books to get an idea of both the numbers of books and what the popular subjects are. Subjects range from the most basic books for the computer illiterate to the most sophisticated books for the computer professional.

Selling a book is similar to selling a magazine article: The publisher does not want to see your unsolicited manuscript, and it is not wise to write the book before making arrangements for its sale, although it might be helpful to write a chapter or two. Follow the same general procedure as in writing an article:

1. Start with a well-defined idea and a well-defined reader (market). That is, decide whether the book is to be for the novice, the experienced computer user, the expert user, or the computer professional.
2. Develop your idea into a detailed, chapter-by-chapter outline, designed to meet the objective.
3. Write a proposal, explaining all of this.
4. Send out copies of your proposal to appropriate publishers. (It is okay to send your proposal to more than one publisher, although most publishers want to be advised of "simultaneous submissions.")

Browsing the computer bookshelves in a few well-stocked bookstores will help you compile a short list of those publishers who seem to be most suitable for the book you want to write. The yellow pages of the publishing world, the *Literary Marketplace* (or LMP), can provide you with the names, addresses, and telephone numbers of computer publishers—broken down by specialty or even geographic region. Your local library probably has a copy.

It is quite possible that some publisher will want to see a sample chapter or two, and it won't hurt to explain in your proposal that these are available. Probably you will want to send the first two or three chapters, if you have written that many. (One rather shrewd editor I met asked me to provide him with my second or third chapter as a sample. "Anyone can write a first chapter," he explained!)

Payment for such books is typically on a royalty basis; the author is paid 10 to 15 percent of the publisher's receipts on the book, usually on a semi-annual basis. Typically, the publisher pays the author an advance against those royalties, usually based on the publisher's worst estimate of sales and appreciation of the production and first-printing cost. With an unknown author, admittedly, the estimate of sales and the advance offered tend to be distinctly on the low side. Still, it can be well worthwhile.

Doing it yourself

All the foregoing is based on the assumption of selling your expert knowledge and services to others who will handle all matters of production and marketing, paying you fees for your contribution of original ideas and designs. Ideally, you will not have sold them all rights to your creations, but will have licensed them to sell your creations and services on a royalty basis. The significant difference is that they are not free to sell your ideas and designs under other arrangements than those you agreed to originally. You have not relinquished your basic rights to your ideas and designs. It is an important distinction, and you must understand it.

Be careful, when signing agreements to permit others to market your services and designs, that you are *licensing* others to sell *your* copyrighted property, and that they acquire no ownership in them thereby. You might decide later to market these special services and products yourself.

Your own products

Many consultants have done well creating and selling a line of products. I recall being invited by a friend to attend a seminar given by a rather well-known consultant and public speaker who pitched his own set of audiotapes, neatly packaged in a case together with a supporting manual, as a part of his presentation. He charged $250 for the package, in addition to the normal seminar fee, and took orders, with payment, for fulfillment, since he had only the demonstration set with him. He managed to sell about $6,000 worth of those sets to even that relatively small assembly of people.

Audiotapes

Should you decide to create an audiotape set to sell, consider going to a professional studio for help in creating the tapes. Even if you are an accomplished public speaker, you can do a better job of turning out a product that is of good commercial quality with professional help. It can take hours of work for each tape, just to record it in a studio. The professionals will then edit and dub music into the leader and trailer, and will probably make other suggestions to help you turn out a polished product.

There are some studios that go well beyond making the tapes for you. Many can even help you with the packaging and accompanying literature. There are even services to help you market your product, since seminars ought not to be the only means of distribution you have if you decide to venture into a product line of your own.

Producing useful publications that you can sell at seminars and elsewhere is even easier than producing tapes for sale. For one thing, it requires less investment and is much easier to do with a PC and laser printer.

Newsletters   The newsletter is a key item. Not only is it an excellent marketing and promotional device, as remarked on earlier, but it can be itself highly profitable. It usually pays its own way and can produce extra income for you, and it supports everything else you do, making your other services and products more profitable.

Monographs   There are many advantages to publishing monographs and other types of brief articles or reports. They may be bound individually and separately as independent publications. They may be completely unpretentious, neatly printed on white 8½-×-11-inch paper and bound with a corner staple. (See FIGS. 7-2 and 7-3.)

Some publishers of such material use covers as an added touch. I have not found this to be absolutely necessary for mail-order sales to individuals, but if you plan to sell these in the back of the room at seminars, an attractive cover or report binder is probably a good idea. Monographs need not be lengthy. In fact, the whole idea is that each deals with a single, specific subject, so most are from 4 to 10 pages, at most. (Some consultants do produce much lengthier reports, bound more formally, but these are not monographs.)

The number of reports you can produce this way is almost without limit. Select topics related to your clients and your prospective clients. That is, you might have a series on database management, another on programming tips and shortcuts, and still another on LANs.

Such reports tend to be priced from about $5 to $8 per report. That might seem high for a few pages offering 2,000 to 5,000 words, but remember that these are not books that will gather dust. You are selling information and expertise, not paper and binding, and these prices are on the conservative side.

Books   Many people self-publish entire books, not because they can't find a commercial publisher for them, but because they prefer to publish the material themselves.

A book can be published in the same manner as reports, on 8½-×-11-inch white paper, printed on one or both sides, and bound in some simple binding, such as with side stitches (staples), 18-hole plastic "combs," or other binder—even in three-ring binders. They can be relatively inexpensive, especially if you do your own typesetting and binding, and have only the printing and collation of pages done by the printer. You can also have your book printed and bound as a paperback with a *perfect* (glued) binding. It makes a presentable book, and is far less costly than *cloth binding* (hard covers).

HERMAN HOLTZ

P.O. Box 1731   Wheaton, MD 20915   (301) 649-2499 Fax: 301 649-5745

GOVERNMENT MARKETS FOR CONSULTANTS

by Herman Holtz

The government, with its hundreds of agencies and thousands of offices, is a multibillion-dollar market for every kind of writing conceivable, and most of it is done under contract by private organizations and often by individuals.

A BASIC ORIENTATION

The 34,000 U.S. Government offices and other facilities scattered throughout the United States and our possessions are spending about $200 billion per year, at current budget rates, for a wide variety of goods and services, many of them expert and consulting services. They call for the services of experts in engineering, management, writing, training, construction, real estate, insurance, and just about every other trade, craft, and profession.

That running the government calls for a great deal of work is well known. What is not so well known is that most of this work does not take place in government offices; the government contracts out most of this work to private industry, including independent consultants (although they do not always identify this work as consulting).

For consultants, the constant growth of new developments and government bureaucracy add up to constantly growing markets. Virtually every government agency of significant size and importance has variety of responsibilities. In many cases, the agency may even have special departments or offices dedicated to activities based largely on outside help of various kinds.

The military organizations who buy the weapons systems and all the related equipment and systems require a great many technical manuals and other documentation to be used to support the training of military personnel and the day to day operations and maintenance of the systems, so they are normally by far the largest developers of publications. However, they are not the only purchaser of such publications, for the National Aviation and Space Administration (NASA), the Environmental Protection Agency (EPA), and many other agencies, such as the Postal Service, also require such documentation.

Training responsibilities may include the development of materials to be used for training, or training materials may be developed by a publications group. There is no set standard in government organization; each agency has a large degree of freedom in organizing itself internally and allocating necessary functions. Each agency does so according to the needs of its own missions, size, and problems. In fact, several agencies--the Internal Revenue Service, the Postal Service, and the Occupational Safety and Health Administration, to name three, have entire training institutes--residential institutions--of their own.

Training

In addition to that, the Office of Personnel Management (formerly the Civil Service Commission), operates a training division with six branches of training, offering training courses to the rest of the federal government. The military agencies have by far the largest training establishments: That

< 131 >

7-2 *A monograph.*

HERMAN HOLTZ

P.O. Box 1731   Wheaton, MD 20915   (301) 649-2499

HOW TO WIN
U.S. GOVERNMENT CONTRACTS

by Herman Holtz

Ask any experienced proposal writer for the secrets of success in Government marketing and the chances are that you will get something such as this:

Never bid a job you know nothing about before seeing it in the *Commerce Business Daily*. You can't win without advance marketing, etc.

Watch your proposal cosmetics--typing, reproduction, covers, margins, and other such details.

25 percent or more of the contracts are wired in advance. You haven't got a chance for these.

Don't bid if you haven't got an advance "understanding" with the customer.

That's the essence of conventional wisdom about proposal writing and Government contracting--and it's right, for most cases. But not for all.

It's right for the average situation, where the proposal writers are just that--proposal writers. What that means is that most proposal writers do a workmanlike job; they present a sound plan by a qualified bidder at a reasonable price. Just that and nothing more But that's not enough:

Many of the other bidders do as much. Many submit proposals that are competent, acceptable, and essential equal to each other. A decision to select one is usually difficult, and other considerations than being competent--being good enough--usually drive the final decision.

In short, *none* of the proposals, in most contract competitions, are truly superior--not inspired by nor based on superior strategies, none truly clever in either concept or execution, none *demanding* attention and somehow dominating the field.

Once in a while, such a proposal appears, and the apple cart is upset. Wired procurements become unwired. The "rules" dictated by that conventional wisdom become irrelevant--bad advice. A dark-horse bidder wins unexpectedly, a competitor who ignored the rules advocated by the experts and ran off with the prize.

At the risk of bragging, I must defend my thesis by telling you this: In writing proposals that have won over $300 million in government contracts for my former employers, clients, and my own account, I have almost always learned of the solicitation through the *Commerce Business Daily*, with no advance work and so "special arrangements." I won each of these on the basis of a proposal that the customer believed merited the award.

7-3 *A brief article.*

Counseling & training

A large part of consulting in any field involves counseling and training clients in whatever special knowledge you have. Seminars have become the most popular means of delivering instruction to groups in the business world where the instruction is on a relatively short-term basis of a few hours or, at most, a few days.

A large part of my own consulting practice has always been presenting training seminars in proposal writing. The methodology I use is not peculiar to proposal writing, however. It is equally useful for conducting seminars in computer programming, database management, or almost anything that a client might want you to teach him or her to do. You can make speaking a key element in your consulting practice, both as a source of income and as a means of marketing the other services or products you provide.

For some extroverts, public speaking is a stimulating and enjoyable experience. For most of us, though, it is a scary prospect. There is something formidable about having a large number of people in an audience before you, all eyes and ears focused on you, seemingly waiting for you to do something embarrassing. It's a common enough fear, and it assails even the bravest.

Many books have been written advising many ways of overcoming this fear of speaking—"platform fever." Most people who manage to persuade themselves to conquer their fears and learn to speak publicly do eventually lose their fear and enjoy the experience each time. Of course, some individuals never lose their fear, but that does not necessarily prevent them from speaking. They approach the podium again and again, even if they do have to conquer the butterflies in their stomachs anew each time.

Overcoming fear of public speaking

Most people can learn to relax on the dais and even come to enjoy making presentations after a few successful experiences. Here are some simple aids to overcoming your fears and lessening the pressures when you first undertake to speak to an audience:

- Begin by reading prepared presentations, preferably short ones not more than 15 to 30 minutes long.
- Get your early experience as a member of a panel of presenters.
- Speak sitting down behind a table or standing behind a lectern.
- Use as many aids as possible—slides, tapes, posters, charts—to focus attention away from you personally.

There are many places and occasions for speaking to audiences. Serving on committees and in organizations will undoubtedly create opportunities to speak at meetings, conventions, symposia, and other such occasions. But it is easy enough to get yourself invited to speak as a guest at others' seminars and courses of instruction. You can also develop and present your own seminars, either for the public or for special groups. Check with your local community college, also. Most are perpetually in search of speakers who can present special classes, courses, and seminars in their adult education programs. You will probably be pleasantly surprised by the warm welcome your offers will get. (Study the current literature your community college publishes to get an idea of how they do this and the kinds of programs offered.)

In many of these activities, such as lecturing at community colleges, you get paid some small fee. The fee is not the point, however. As with other PR activities, it would probably pay you to make the presentations without compensation of any kind.

You do not have to become an outstanding orator to be a success on the platform. There are many simple things you can do that help make your presentations successful. Following are a few of the things that I do to help capture and hold the attention of audiences:

- Enunciate each word clearly.
- Smile a great deal (when smiling is appropriate).
- Look people in the eye, moving your gaze about frequently.
- Encourage questions and comments from the audience.
- Be enthusiastic, and unrestrained in showing it.

That last item is most important. Enthusiasm is contagious, and it adds incalculable interest to your presentation. You must demonstrate your enthusiasm: Ask rhetorical questions loudly and answer them in an audible whisper. Ask rhetorical questions in an audible whisper and answer them loudly. Get out from behind the lectern. Move about the platform. Invade the audience. Wave your arms. Grimace. Shout. Whisper. Roll your eyes. You might be amazed at how big a hand you will get from your audience when you conclude. More importantly, they will remember you and tell others about you.

Seminars

The seminar is best suited to teaching a single, special subject, such as the latest version of WordPerfect, or some class of programs such as databases or spreadsheets. In fact, what the seminar is best suited for is almost identical with the nature of consulting—specialized knowledge and skills.

Seminars are traditionally used for advanced instruction, studies, and discussions involving graduate students. Today, many people also use seminars to serve as introductory courses in many fields. Most seminars are one day long, which means about six hours of instruction: three in the morning and three in the afternoon. That might be a heavy load to put on both the presenter—assuming that you present alone, as most of us do—and the attendees, especially if the subject is a "heavy" one. One way around that problem is to present the subject as a series of shorter seminars of a half-day or even of an hour or two. The *Training* magazine annual trade show, for example, usually features a series of half-day seminars for attendees.

At the other extreme is the longer seminar, several days' length. It usually lasts six hours a day with evening frivolities for the attendees, who need relaxation after a strenuous six hours of lectures, demonstrations, and exercises of various kinds.

However long or short it is, the typical seminar is a very focused event, often presenting more information than most people can absorb in the time allotted. For that reason alone, if for no other, a seminar ought to include a generous supply of handout materials that document the important matter of the seminar for the attendee to review and digest at leisure.

The outline of a one-day seminar in consulting is presented in FIG. 7-4, a reproduction of part of the brochure announcing the seminar and soliciting registrations.

Handouts A special seminar manual makes an ideal handout, and I developed such a manual for my seminar on proposal writing. However, that was a seminar I presented often enough to make it reasonable to dedicate the time for writing such a substantial manual. Some seminar presenters charge the attendee or the sponsor a per-copy price for seminar manuals. I prefer not to. When I do a sponsored seminar—the only kind I do today—I give the sponsor a single master copy of the camera-ready copy and permission to duplicate and bind as many copies as are required for the seminar.

For the occasional seminar, it is not always practical to write a formal manual as a handout. However, there are many alternatives. You can develop a series of sheets to be handed out at appropriate points in your presentation. If you use transparencies with an overhead projector, you might find it useful to make printed copies of these and hand them out, for example. Or, if graphs, tables, and matrices are appropriate to your presentation, you might hand out copies of these.

In many cases you can get handouts for free. I have been able to get many government publications to hand out to my audiences in seminars on proposal writing and other aspects of marketing to government agencies. Many private organizations—corporations and associations—also have publications they will happily supply free to be distributed to your attendees. It is likely that IBM, Microsoft, and others will be happy to oblige.

Marketing seminars There are two basic avenues for selling seminar presentations as a consulting service. One is the open registration approach, where you produce your own seminar.

First you develop the seminar for the audience you anticipate, and you prepare all the materials you will need. Then you make arrangements for the meeting room (usually in a local hotel but sometimes in some other public place that can provide meeting space). Then you advertise it to induce prospective attendees to register. If you are advertising to the general public, public media—newspaper, newsletter, and radio-TV advertising—will do, but if you are after a special group, you must turn to direct mail.

Proposals for Government Contracts
How to Develop Winning Proposals

8:30 a.m. - REGISTRATION, coffee and pastries
9:00 a.m. - Session Begins

I. The $160 Billion Market
  a. Understanding the market
  b. What the government buys
  c. How to sell to the government.

II. Locating Sales Opportunities
  a. How to uncover selling opportunities.
  b. Getting on the appropriate bidder's list.
  c. How to use the *Commerce Business Daily* as an effective marketing tool.
  d. How to use the Freedom of Information Act to market.

III. Proposal Strategy Development
  a. Why proposals?
  b. What is a proposal?
  c. What does the customer want?
  d. What must the proposal do?
  e. What makes a winner?
  f. Why strategy makes the difference.

IV. The Stages of Proposal Development
  a. Bid/no-bid analysis and decision.
  b. Requirement analysis—understanding the requirements.
  c. Indentification of the critical factor(s).
  d. Formulation of the approach and technical/program/pricing strategies.
  e. Formulation of the capture strategy.
  f. Establishing the theme.
  g. Design and presentation strategy.
  h. Writing the proposal.

V. Persuasive Proposal Writing
  a. What is persuasion?
  b. The art of persuasive writing.
  c. What makes others agree?
  d. What turns them on? And off?

VI. How to Write a Winning Proposal
  a. Writing to communicate.
  b. Writing to sell.
  c. Writing to arouse and sustain interest.
  d. Your proposal should promise desirable end-results.
  e. Your proposal should, preferably, be a unique claim, one your competitors can't match.
  f. Your proposal must be able to prove it's validity.

VII. Formats and Proposal Content
  a. Recommended format.
  b. Front matter and other elements.
  c. How to use format for best results.

VIII. Cost Justification in Proposals
  a. Understanding costs.
  b. What the government expects in cost proposals.
  c. Technical vs. cost proposal.
  d. Construction of the quote.
  e. How to make bids.

WHO SHOULD ATTEND: If you are a small business executive and would like your company to increase its sales or profits in the enormous government market, or if you're a marketing executive in a major corporation, this seminar will be of tremendous benefit to you. New employees will shorten their learning curve. This seminar is designed to benefit marketing executives, contract administrators, engineers, systems analysts, computer specialists, trainers, editors, proposal writers, accountants, lawyers, contract specialists, manufacturers, service companies, consultants, and individuals seeking government contracts. Our faculty's expert advice has helped companies win contracts worth $1 million to $25 million and that expertise can be yours by attending this fact-filled seminar. Just one tip or one idea can be worth thousands of dollars to you.

MATERIALS: Each participant will receive an exclusive Handbook on Proposalmanship, authored by Herman Holtz, along with a host of other valuable materials.

7-4 *An outline for a one-day seminar.*

This type of seminar is time-consuming and laborious, but highly profitable, if successful. Moreover, depending on the services or products you offer and the kind of attendees you attract, it is also an excellent route to win new clients. Many seminar attendees, if pleased with the presentation and impressed with you, will seek you out for further business. Not only is each attendee your client for the duration of the seminar, some might become repeat clients.

Another way to market seminars is as a service to individual clients. That is, you can present custom seminars to various clients. I have presented seminars to the staffs of various companies, for example, under contract to the company. I provide the program, ordinarily customized to the company by adapting my standard general seminars to the special interests of the client. (I learned early that the cost of creating custom seminars from scratch was prohibitive, and clients would not pay the bill for that.) I charge the company, my client, a flat fee plus expenses for my work. (Some presenters charge the client a fee for each attendee.) This is a workable marketing plan with many clients, including professional or trade associations, universities, corporations, and many others.

There is still another marketing approach, a hybrid of the foregoing two methods. In this approach you are sponsored by an organization that does all the marketing and charges attendees registration and attendance fees. The organization may solicit registrations or not, depending on their own mission and mode of operation, and they might offer you a flat fee or a fee plus a percentage.

Seminar tips

Producing and presenting seminars deserves serious consideration. Here are a few tips and reminders to keep in mind:

- A typical day's session runs approximately six hours, three in the morning and three in the afternoon, with midmorning and midafternoon breaks of about 10 minutes. The lunch break is usually from 90 minutes to two hours.
- Software and publications are often sold at seminars in what are called "back-of-the-room" sales. Many seminar presenters say they normally create as much income from such sales as they do from attendance fees, and they attach great importance to this aspect of their seminars and other public speaking. Back-of-the-room sales may be conducted prior to the start of the morning session, during the lunch break, and after the close of the afternoon session. They should not be conducted during the presentations.
- Whether you sell books, tapes, or other materials, you should include handout materials as part of the seminar. These are themselves often a major inducement to registration and attendance. It helps, from that viewpoint, if they are available only to registered attendees.
- In many cases you can get excellent materials free from government agencies, associations, community groups, large corporations, schools, and other sources. You might also be able to get speakers free of charge from such sources. As a computer consultant, you should always consider asking local computer dealers and others in the computer business for any such support—that is, speakers and handout materials.
- Visual aids—movies, slides, film strips, transparencies, and posters of various kinds—are also available from such sources as those just named.
- One rather profitable idea is the mini-seminar. I held these two- to three-hour sessions for 10 to 15 people in my offices on Saturday mornings,

charging what was even then a rather modest fee—$25. If your office at home is unsuitable for this purpose, you can usually arrange to rent an inexpensive room somewhere.

- A variant on the previous idea is to conduct two such sessions, one in the morning, another in the afternoon, enabling yourself to register twice the number of attendees for a single day. (The total cost is only slightly greater for two sessions, and the income is, of course, doubled.)

Training courses

Training need not be done by seminars. You can also conduct training courses in a series of one- or two-hour nightly or weekend courses. You can organize these on your own and advertise them in the local papers, or you can make arrangements with a local college.

Most community colleges run extensive adult-education courses, and are always eager to get new courses and instructors. The pay is usually less than munificent, but there are also the marketing benefits to derive. If you choose your subjects with care, you will attract some students who can become clients, or provide word-of-mouth advertising to potential clients.

Consulting via writing

Writing offers you another means for providing a special kind of consulting service, both similar to and different from doing it as a speaker. It is a kind of group consulting that also enables you to offer some limited one-on-one consulting. One way to do this is via a regular column in some periodical.

For example, Craig Crossman writes a weekly computer question-and-answer column syndicated to a number of newspapers via the Knight-Ridder syndicate. In answering reader's queries about computers, Crossman is furnishing one-on-one consulting, but making the service available to all. In one recent column, Crossman tells one reader how to speed up response from a CD ROM using disk-caching software. Crossman also hosts a national radio program, in which he does the same kind of thing, and also interviews authors of relevant books.

Obviously, not everyone can write a nationally syndicated column about computers, but you might be able to do a column for some local paper or perhaps for someone's newsletter.

Products in consulting

Consulting is generally considered to be a service offered clients. Yet, many PC consultants deal in products as well as services. The industry is still in a dynamic stage, changing and growing swiftly, with an almost constant stream of new and improved products urging the early obsolescence of existing products. Many clients look to their PC consultants for guidance or, at least, respond to the consultants' offers of guidance in keeping their systems up to date.

Thus you might be a dealer in computer hardware and software, or you even a manufacturer of software, as some PC consultants are. Some consultants also become publishers, producing monographs, manuals, audiotape sets, and even videotapes for sale. Major hardware items are normally sold to clients via one-on-one sales presentations, probably most often to existing clients.

John Parker, owner of Megabyte Computer Services, sells hardware occasionally, although it is a minor part of his business, he says. Still, when a client wishes to buy through him, Parker can profit from the sale. Selling hardware to his clients is an accommodation for the client, and serves Parker as a marketing tool.

Profile: Writing & speaking

Raj Khera uses writing and speaking as powerful tools both to produce income and build awareness of his home-based consultancy, Khera Communications, Inc. He offers a whole range of products—including seminars, audiotapes, and a monthly newsletter—in addition to more traditional technical writing and consulting services.

Producing a seminar

Khera put together his first seminar inspired by books on consulting he'd read and memories of his college days, when he gave talks on managing stress to student groups. Khera designs his seminars very methodically. First, he decides what facet of his business he wants to emphasize. Next, he determines his target audience, asking himself who would want to hear a message on that topic. Then, he finds an organization that has such an audience, contacts the program director, and offers to come speak. Most of the time, he reports, the response is, "Sure! How soon can you come?"

Khera speaks primarily to PC user's groups, conventions, and conferences such as a recent Independent Computer Consultants Association meeting in New York (where he got 23 qualified leads from among the attendees, several of whom have become clients). Attendees at his seminars get a sample of Khera's newsletter and are asked to fill out an evaluation form about the seminar. Khera concentrates his back-of-the-room efforts on collecting these evaluations and business cards, rather than selling other products. This fits with his goal of adding qualified prospects to his marketing database and getting positive feedback to use (with permission, of course) in later marketing efforts.

Khera says he was surprised at first by how often seminar attendees become clients. As he puts it, "Go onstage, show people how not to use you, and they'll use you!"

Producing a tape

The contents of Khera's first audiotape came from a seminar he gave to a user's group. He explains, "I taped the seminar, so just in case it came out really good, I could sell it. The seminar went great, but the sound quality was bad, so I sat in my basement and gave the seminar again to my tape recorder."

Khera is better-equipped than most PC consultants to produce an audiotape. As an amateur musician, he already has a small recording studio in his basement. Still, he says, "You don't really need a lot of equipment—just a good tape deck and microphone."

Once the first tape was edited and an introduction added by a friend with a good speaking voice (reading a script Khera wrote), Khera looked into having it reproduced professionally. Deciding he could not justify that expense, especially with an unknown product, Khera decided to produce them himself in small batches of 20 or 30 at a time. He buys blank tapes and cases in bulk at a discount and prints out packaging on his laser printer using Avery audio labels. The result, he says, "is a professional job at minimal cost."

Khera markets the tapes primarily through press releases and seminars. So far, they are not a major source of income, but that is not their purpose for his business. Instead, he uses them as an effective "awareness tool" to leave with hot prospects.

Producing a newsletter

Khera started his newsletter, *The Khera Business Report* (shown in FIG. 7-5), as a free service to his target audience of PC consultants. However, demand quickly became so great that he began to charge $59 for an annual subscription, and now has subscribers throughout the world.

The four-page newsletter is produced monthly, with two special annual issues on computer consulting rates and marketing practices. Most of the material comes from surveys he takes and a syndicated column he writes, so producing the newsletter takes relatively little time. Khera says the newsletter succeeds because it presents "very condensed information. One of my clients said how glad he was to be able to digest it all in just a few minutes. Most of the information is already out there; I'm just helping cope with the information overload."

Producing a proposal

While Khera finds newsletters and audiotapes are useful "leave-behinds" after meeting with prospective clients, he relies primarily on written proposals to close his sales. Khera always submits proposals within 48 hours of meeting with prospects, even if they do not request one. His standard, five-page proposal includes the following:

- Background of the project
- Objective of the project
- Supporting information (who he'll interview, what operating systems and programs are involved, etc.)
- Suggested approach (his capabilities and the general way he would work)
- Delivery schedule
- Cost

FEBRUARY 1993

PROFIT-MAKING STRATEGIES FOR HIGH TECHNOLOGY BUSINESSES

the khera business report

PUBLISHED BY *Khera Communications, Inc.*, GAITHERSBURG, MARYLAND

Quotable Quotes

"If you find a good solution and become attached to it, the solution may become your next problem."

- Robert Anthony

"What lies behind us and what lies before us are tiny matters compared to what lies within us."

- Oliver Wendell Holmes

In the next issue:

Getting the Most Out of Your Documentation (and Other Written Material)

National Survey:
Current Marketing Practices of Computer Firms

And More!

If you don't receive *The Khera Business Report*, call (301) 309-0969 right now. Don't miss the next issue!

The 1993 Economic Outlook for Computer Service Firms

"In 1993, all information services subsectors are projected to experience positive real growth rates higher than those of the national economy," according to the 1993 U.S. Industrial Outlook released in January by the International Trade Administration (ITA) of the Commerce Department. The report profiles foreign and domestic prospects for over 350 industries. Although growth is not expected to reach levels stated in past reports, a promising 1993 is projected as part of the national economic recovery.

So, just what are the prospects for the coming year? Very much like last year, the best opportunities are for UNIX application programmers, electronic data interchange (EDI) systems managers, computer trainers who have foreign language abilities, consultants and systems analysts with international marketing experience, and local area network (LAN) integrators. The decrease in the availability of venture capital has reduced the size, rather than the number, of start-up firms offering computer services.

The projections in the report are based on studies by ITA staff and market research companies including Input, Dataquest, and International Data Corporation. Here are more specific projections broken down into five different consulting areas:

Data Processing. Defined broadly as transaction processing and electronic data interchange, this sector of the computer industry grew 13% in 1992, right on target with the 13.5% predicted growth cited in last year's report. Transaction processing services include medical and

(See page 2 - OUTLOOK)

The Khera Business Report is a copyrighted publication. Duplication of the material in this publication is strictly prohibited. Please honor our intellectual property rights. Thank you.

7-5 *The first page of Raj Khera's monthly newsletter (used with permission).*

At the end of the proposal, he includes a very simple letter of agreement for the prospects to sign and return within 10 days if they would like him to begin work. He follows up the proposal with a telephone call in another two or three days.

Khera has found this approach to be extremely successful, estimating a 75 to 80 percent success rate. He admits to being burned at first, though, by giving away too much information in the proposal. Now he is more careful, particularly in the "suggested approach" section.

Khera advises, "Getting a proposal in their hands within 48 hours is critical. The quality of the proposal and the other material you leave behind is also important. When your clients tell you that your competitors might be cheaper, but you're more professional, you know you're doing it right."

8 Rates, negotiations, & contracts

Successful home-based PC consulting means understanding and accepting that what you are doing is a business, and must be conducted in a thoroughly businesslike manner with full appreciation of business realities.

Some consultants charge the same rates for every job, small or large, difficult or easy. However, there is the matter of the larger assignment, the assignment that might keep you busy every workday for a number of months. Should you—can you—charge the same rates for that kind of job that you do for the small job? Others will discount their rates for the large job. In fact, the client with a large job to award might very well take the position that he or she is entitled to a discounted rate because the job is a large one, and insist that you lower your normal rate if you want the job.

That demand is not entirely unreasonable. Ordinarily, your overhead drops sharply when you undertake the large job because your unbillable time is usually a major part of your overhead, whether it is idle time or time spent marketing. If you are like most independent consultants working on small jobs most of the time, you must spend from one-fourth to one-third of your time in marketing, administrative chores, and other unbillable time. Getting a long-term assignment with a guaranteed 40 hours billable every week for a number of months cuts a large chunk out of your overhead for that period of time. You should thus be able to cut your rates a bit—perhaps 10 to 20

Rates & variables

percent—without losing money. You might find it necessary to have two rate scales: one for the typical small job, and another for the long-term job.

Rates for brokers

Some 25 percent of independent computer consultants turn to brokers for much of their work, and others use brokers occasionally. This is a subcontracting situation; the broker has contracted with an end-client, a consumer of consulting services, and satisfies that contractual obligation by awarding subcontracts to independents such as you. Here you encounter another common problem. It is, in fact, a rather common scenario:

> A broker calls PC consultant Harry B. to offer Harry a subcontract on a labor-hour assignment at a client's premises. He asks a few routine questions about Harry's qualifications and availability, and then asks, in the same matter-of-fact tone, "What are you getting now?"

Harry is taken unawares. He is still rather new at conducting his own consulting practice and perhaps even somewhat naive, especially regarding how some brokers do business. And so he answers immediately, as a reflex, that he has been charging his clients $40 an hour. The response from the broker is, "Good. No problem. I'll get back to you."

Now that Harry has a few minutes to reflect, he is disturbed and feels that he has been trapped. (Harry isn't *that* inexperienced!) He knows that his rate is far too low for what he does. He has been charging that low rate only to make it easier to get his first few clients. He knows that the broker will charge the client at least double that rate. He realizes that he should have gotten at least $50 an hour, and could probably have gotten more than that. Now he has lost his bargaining chip, he fears, and is stuck with that low rate forever, with this broker, at least.

All too often, especially when PC consultants are not yet heavily experienced, they set a price and find the other party agrees too readily. Immediately, they suspect that they "left money on the table," i.e., asked for much less than they could have gotten. Then again, the other's apparent acceptance might not be acceptance at all. An unblinking nod and murmur does not necessarily signify acceptance. The other might simply not be ready to discuss money and negotiate or might want you to start feeling smug and complacent!

Harry now wants to know how he should have answered that question without lying, which he is reluctant to do. He also wants to know if there is any way he can salvage the current situation and regain a bargaining position so that he doesn't, in the end, leave a lot of money on the table.

Fielding the question

The answer to the first question, how to respond to a request for information on how much you are getting, is to refuse to furnish that kind of information to a broker (or even to a client). What you are getting now is neither the broker's business nor germane to the situation. Of course, you don't want to offend the broker or the client, so you don't say, "It's none of your business." You can find more diplomatic ways to be responsive without undercutting your negotiating position or lying.

One way to do this is to simply say, "I want *X* dollars an hour," or "My current rate is *X*." Since this is the opening of a bargaining situation or negotiation, you normally stipulate the highest possible rate, preferably a bit higher than the maximum you believe you can get—but not exorbitantly higher, if you want to negotiate. If you are too far out in left field with your initial position, the other party might decide immediately that there is no use trying to negotiate with you.

There is yet another way to handle this, a way that may give you some advantage: Refuse to respond when the question is asked, again in a nondefiant, diplomatic way. Say something like, "I can discuss the question of rates a lot better after I get more information on the assignment and decide what it entails and whether I want it." Follow that up with questions about where the work is to be done, what the hours are to be, how long the assignment will last, and a dozen other details.

There are specific advantages to you in handling the question this way:

- You gain the high ground psychologically by making it clear that you are not leaping at the job, and might not accept it at all.
- You might find that the other party is suddenly on the defensive and trying to sell you on taking the job, when until now he or she thought you were eager to reach an agreement.
- You should, in fact, find out what all the "warts" of the job are before you indicate you are ready to accept it (as you do by stating a rate you will accept). Some of those warts might be grounds for getting a premium rate. For example, the work might require travel or extensive commuting, an uncomfortable workplace, a client known to be difficult, late hours, or work you prefer not to do.

Setting the rate

At this point, the considerations for setting your rate are not greatly different for a broker than for any other client. If you are entirely businesslike, as you should be, you and the business are different entities. The business is paying you a salary, and trying to earn a profit above that salary. You apply the same logic in quoting rates to a broker that you do in quoting directly to a client.

You try to get the highest rate, and you negotiate, giving up as little as possible, but recognizing the realities of the situation and compromising as necessary.

Asking clients the right questions

Here are some routine questions you need to get answers for in all cases before setting a rate:

1. Where is the workplace?
2. If travel or heavy commuting is required, what are the provisions for expenses? Will they be actual or fixed per diem?
3. Will there be overtime? If so, at what rates, relative to the base rate, and how much is anticipated?
4. How long is the assignment to last? Are there minimum or maximum guarantees?
5. How fast can I expect my invoices to be paid? (This, because it concerns the question of your cash flow, can be an important factor to you.)
6. Are there any special conditions?

The answers to some of these might spawn other questions, but you can see the significance of these. More to the point, you can see the need to get this information before you agree to any rate.

A fixed price as an alternative to a rate

For some reason, computer consultants tend to set rates based on an hourly figure. That mindset is probably the result of so many computer consultants hiring on to work on the clients' premises as technical temporaries. And that is the result of so many clients wanting computer consultants to work in that manner, with no clearly defined end-product to be created and delivered, but simply to work on whatever needs doing at the moment.

Aside from any other considerations, such an open-ended hourly arrangement can cause tax problems. The IRS is looking closely at whether the consultants hired on this basis are actually employees. Part of the IRS's decision involves, how a consultant charges (hourly or fixed) and whether there is a definite deliverable. (The complete list of questions is in chapter 9.) If the IRS decides you are an employee, you lose the tax benefits of self-employment, but probably don't gain any of the benefits of regular employment. This, in itself, is a good reason to set fixed prices.

Small jobs   Some computer consultants take on only small jobs, such as installing personal computers in small offices, installing software, training office personnel in computer usage, running small seminars in popular types of software, and other tasks that run to an hour, a half-day, or a few days only. Probably most consultants would charge by the hour for such work, but it is possible to have a scale of fixed prices for such jobs, if you prefer. It is necessary to charge "portal to portal"—travel time—or to set your rates high enough to compensate you for travel when you handle small jobs. In this kind of practice, travel is a major element of the time you must spend. One advantage to this type of work is that you can build a clientele who will call on you again and again as their needs arise.

Projects   Perhaps your work consists of relatively lengthy projects, running to many days, weeks, or longer. Where it is possible to define a project in terms of an end-product that can be specified, and you can estimate with some confidence just how much time, effort, materials, and other expenses are required to complete the project, you can set a fixed price for the job. There is a bit of risk in that, of course, but you can minimize it if you are quite careful in making your estimate and writing up your bid or proposal.

Be sure to quantify everything, not only the hours and dollars you must provide, but the end-product: the lines of code, number of pages, number and kinds of illustrations, or whatever else is necessary, both qualitatively and quantitatively. Then you have a "place to stand" if the client makes additional demands when you have completed the project. You can demonstrate that you have delivered what you contracted to deliver. It is essential to do this, if you are to avoid disputes that you would almost surely lose.

Negotiations

We negotiate all our lives, although we don't always call it that. In principle, negotiating is simply stating what you want, while the other party states what he or she wants, and then trying to reach a compromise that both of you are satisfied with and can agree to. In practice, it is a far more complex process, to which more than one entire book has been devoted. Knowing how to negotiate is useful to everyone in the business world, necessary to everyone managing a business, and absolutely essential to a home-based PC consultant.

A proper goal of negotiations

Milton Fogelman was a most erudite and charming contracting officer for one of the federal government's agencies. He believed that a contract was not worth anything if one of the parties to it was dissatisfied and resentful, believing that he or she had been hammered into a one-sided agreement. He therefore always listened carefully and patiently to what the other party had to say during the negotiations, no matter how protracted those negotiations were. He always responded in some way to objections or other comments made by the other party. And he never concluded a negotiation, even when agreement had been reached, without asking the other party if he or she was truly satisfied that the agreement was an equitable one.

His theory was that no contract is a good one if it is not entered into in good faith by both parties. It's a good philosophy. You will almost surely have problems with the other party and the contract if you enter into a contract in which either of you feels victimized to even a small extent.

Thus the objective of any negotiation ought to be an agreement you and your client enter into in good faith and with the conviction that it is a fair bargain. It isn't always easy to do this; perhaps it isn't always possible. Some negotiations are going to fail, under this definition of successful negotiations, even if an agreement is reached. But most of the time, skilled negotiators can manage it.

Principles, tactics, & procedures

There is not room here, of course, for an extensive discussion of the art of negotiating, or all the myriad tactics, techniques, and nuances of skillful negotiating. We can, however, examine a few important principles, some of which you will recognize immediately as familiar tactics in even informal negotiations.

Effective negotiations cannot be rushed You need time to feel out the other party and find out what his or her real needs are, and where he or she is most likely to be vulnerable. You also need time for many kinds of negotiating tactics to be effective.

One reason to slow down the process is to get the other side to invest time in the negotiation. It's easy enough for him or her to say, "Forget it," if you polarize positions immediately with anything that sounds like an ultimatum, or if you appear to be too rushed. Once the other party has invested some time in trying to reach agreement, there is at least some reluctance to waste the investment, and thus some inducement to talk some more and try to reach an agreement. Too, if the other party believes that he or she is in the catbird seat—has an advantage that can be expressed to you as "take it or leave it"—you need to gently dilute that by slowing things down.

Appear to be negotiating from a position of strength Talk as though you have options if this negotiation does not succeed. Suggest, for example, that scheduling can become a problem if you don't get to decision reasonably soon, or say that you need to decide on another possible project. Never make it appear that the negotiation is one-sided and you have no power. The fact that the other party is willing to invest the time to negotiate indicates that he or she does want to do business with you, wants whatever it is that you have to offer. You already know that much. What remains is to decide how much you must yield and how much the other will yield—or can yield.

Simple bargaining might do the trick "I will give a bit if you will give a bit." This is usually reserved for the latter part of a negotiation, when you have reached a point where you are not too far apart. Try first to swap something else for money.

He says, "My boss will skin me alive if I agree to more than $15,000 absolute tops." That is probably a bargain tactic in itself—"I would love to go along, but old so-and-so would never buy it."

You say, "Well, suppose we trim the deliverable a bit. I'll write the code, but no final report and no turnkey installation."

"Oh, no," he says, "I have to have the report and the installation."

Now you have used a good negotiating tactic, and weakened his argument a bit, putting him on the defensive. He grudgingly raises that "maximum" a bit.

Know when to stop   At some point, finally, probably each of you issues an ultimatum, although it doesn't sound like an ultimatum.

She says, "Well, I really can't go above $5,600, and I am going out on a limb with that."

You say, "I don't see how I can go under $6,000 and deliver everything you want."

Now that you are only $400 apart, you can split the difference, perhaps. If the other party is really too stubborn to go a step further and you want the project badly enough, perhaps you can swap something for money, such as, "I'll tell you what: I will do the job for $5,600 if you will make progress payments every month and take not more than a week to pay my invoices."

Thus you reach a successful conclusion, something you could not have done without a negotiation. It takes patience, listening, understanding the other's position and problems, flexibility, and a willingness to compromise.

Contracts

The purpose of negotiation is to reach agreement, of course, and so successful negotiations normally end in contracts. The contract might be a verbal one, especially if the job is small, such as installing some new software or training a client in the use of a fax-modem. Such an agreement would normally result from some quite simple and informal negotiation, beginning with a client's query as to whether you do a particular kind of work, your affirmative answer, and settlement on price, time, and place. This contract may not be a formal, written one, but it is usually wise and in your interest to have all contracts clearly spelled out in writing and duly signed.

The subject of contracts is an inescapable one because PC consultants are independent contractors (unless compelled by the IRS to accept W2 assignments as temporary employees). Being an "IC" (independent contractor) means that you are working under contract, of course. The contract may be verbal only, but unless you work on very small jobs that last only a short time, you are likely to have written contracts—and well-advised to insist on doing so. Written contracts can be quite simple or fairly complex, according to circumstance.

Whether you write your own contracts, have a lawyer write them for you, use boilerplate models from a book or computer program, or operate your consulting practice entirely on verbal agreements, you should understand the law of contracts. That knowledge itself constitutes a good course in business practice, especially when linked to knowledge of the Uniform Commercial Code (discussed shortly).

Major hazards of contracts

Paradoxically enough, the two major hazards of written contracts are having one and not having one. The first is a hazard to sales and marketing, and the second is a hazard to profitable operations. Both need explanation.

The sales and marketing hazard   Many consultants can relate experiences of sales lost because of formidable multipage contracts. Written contracts, unless they are simple letter agreements, often intimidate clients. It is probably unfair to the legal profession generally to characterize lawyers as "deal breakers," as some marketers do, but it is nonetheless true that many lawyers tend to great formality and imposing sheafs of paper when creating a contract. It is, in fact, not the lawyers per se that are the deal breakers, but the *whereases*, *wherefores*, and *formal bindings* that frighten clients and break deals. Those things, combined with the rest of the difficult and arcane language that many lawyers use even today, can result in a formidable document that makes a client exceedingly uneasy and often leads to cancellation of the sale. The thick bundle of pages bound in a blue folder is a "no-no" for you. From the marketing viewpoint, contracts must be written in simple, everyday language, far less forbidding and thus much more acceptable to clients.

Not all formal contracts must be so forbidding. It is possible to execute formal contracts that are relatively simple—even a single page—and yet cover the major points.

The hazards to profitable operation   Operating on any but the simplest and briefest task without a written agreement entails the obvious hazard of disputes and disagreements as to what the requirement was and whether you have met and satisfied the requirement. The chief reason for putting an agreement into writing is to minimize the occurrence of such disputes, and furnish a basis for prompt and direct resolution if such disputes do occur. To paraphrase Murphy's Law, anything a client can misinterpret he or she will misinterpret. That is, anything not specifically spelled out in an agreement is quite likely to be interpreted by the client in his or her favor. You then have a dispute, and it is always difficult to win disputes with clients, unless you are willing to risk a Pyrrhic victory.

Non-compete clauses   The non-compete clause is found in most contracts offered by brokers. This clause bans you from soliciting or accepting assignments directly with any client of the broker's whom you have become acquainted with as a result of subcontracting to the broker—from "stealing" the broker's clients and cutting the broker out. It's understandable that brokers wish to have such a clause, and probably a one-year term (from the end of the assignment) for such a restriction is reasonable, although some consultants insist that they will not agree to more than six months for a non-compete clause. Some brokers might try to persuade you to sign a contract with a two-year inhibition on competing. Think before you agree to this.

Certain basic and specific elements are required by law to make a valid and enforceable contract:

Contract basics

- A valid offer
- An acceptance of the offer
- A valid consideration
- Legal competence of the parties to enter into agreement
- A legal undertaking
- Agreement in writing (in some cases)

Translated, this means one party must offer to do something for the other and provide a consideration (usually money, but not that necessarily); the other must accept the offer; the two parties must be legally capable of contracting (of legal age and sound mind); and the agreement must be to do something that is within the law. Thus a contract entered into by a minor is not valid, nor is a contract to do something illegal, nor is any contract that lacks these basic requirements.

In most cases, verbal contracts are as binding as are written contracts. They are valid and enforceable, although obviously there is the problem of persuading a court that there was agreement on the terms the complaining party reports and claims. There are some exceptions: the Statute of Frauds (the law in all states in the U.S.) requires that contracts referring to matters covered under these statutes be in writing. These are, usually, contracts for interest in land, contracts that are to take effect a year or more after they are drawn up, and contracts pledging responsibility for debts, defaults, or miscarriage of another party. The Uniform Commercial Code (UCC), accepted in each state with the state's own modifications, also requires that certain kinds of contracts be in writing.

The practice of law is far from being an exact science; it is far more art than science. None of the terms describing the basic requirements of all contracts can be stated or measured with precision, which is one of the difficulties. Interpreting what is or is not a "valid consideration," for example, can be the subject of a great deal of dispute. Agreeing to something that is illegal is another problem. The agreement to do something against the law is an invalid contract, but it is not always readily apparent that the agreed-upon service or exchange was against the law.

These points aside, a contract is basically an agreement to make an exchange of something for something else, such as your services for some number of dollars. But it is still not that simple. Just what services are called for? When, where, and how must they be delivered? With what guarantees, if any? How soon must dollars be paid? What are the remedies if one side does not carry out the bargain fully? How can the contract be liquidated if the two parties agree to void it?

Of course, in major contracts, such as those involving millions of dollars, there will be platoons of lawyers involved and a thick contract document resulting. In negotiating a $9.5 million contract with a federal agency, my employer brought 10 people to five days of negotiations, and the number of negotiators was matched by the government. Of course, as an independent consultant, you are not likely to contract on any scale resembling this, and can turn to sources other than lawyers for help.

John Cotton Howell, a retired lawyer of lengthy experience, recommends that self-employed individuals whose contracting needs are simple, learn to write their own contracts, advice echoed by many other lawyers, some retired and others still practicing. There are a number of books to guide you in this, as well as software that will generate contracts tailored to your choices, which you can then take to a lawyer for evaluation, if you wish.

There are different levels for written contracts. A written contract may be a simple, one-page letter of agreement, as shown in FIG. 8-1, or it may be a simple form, such as the purchase order shown in FIG. 8-2. These simple forms will usually serve quite satisfactorily for small, routine consulting tasks, such as installing new software. (I recently had to call on Microsoft's own experts for help in installing DOS 6.0, but they were able to help me with a simple instruction delivered by telephone. A purchase order would have been quite adequate to serve as a contract for this task.)

On the other hand, depending on the nature of your specialty, you are likely to encounter more elaborate projects, such as long-term, on-site assignments. You might win these directly with clients, or with brokers (who hold prime contracts) as a subcontractor. The clients might have their own contracting forms or issue purchase orders, if they are large companies or use consultants frequently. Otherwise, be prepared to furnish your own agreement or contract form. Brokers will probably have their own contracting forms, which they will ask you to sign. As mentioned earlier, scan those carefully and negotiate those clauses you find objectionable.

Examples of formal contracts

There are many types of contracts you are likely to encounter as a computer consultant, aside from the informal Letter of Agreement and purchase orders. The kinds of contracts you are most likely to need depends on the nature of your specialty, of course; few consultants are going to need all types. Some representative examples are shown here.

Service agreement   Figure 8-3 is a relatively simple service agreement. As a model, it includes many clauses that might have to be negotiated with the client. You might encounter these or similar clauses in a client's or broker's standard boilerplate, imprinted in advance in their contract forms. That does not mean that you must accept them, although you would normally be assured that they are "routine," "no problem," or are just

AGREEMENT

Client:

_____
     (Name & address)

*Client
contact*:_____
     (Name of individual)

Services to be provided or relevant specifications/proposal, if applicable:

_____

_____

_____

Reports/presentations:_____

On client's premises [ ]   *On consultant's premises* [ ]

Other or special arrangements:_____

Beginning date:_____   *Target completion date*:_____

Fees: $_____ *per*_____ No._____*Total est. fee/cost*: $_____
    (hr/day/other)   (hr/day other)

Other costs: $_____ (for:_____)

Advance retainer: $_____ *Terms for balance*:_____

_____

Notes, remarks, special provisions, if any:_____

_____

_____

_____

For_____(consultant) For_____(client)
 (type/print)   (type/print)

_____ (signed) _____(signed)

_____ (date) _____(date)

8-1 *Simple letter of agreement.*

necessary "to satisfy the lawyers." (In fact, many lawyers would tend to use much more ornate and all-encompassing language and twice as many pages.) Despite such assurances, study these clauses carefully and decide whether you can accept them as written.

PURCHASE ORDER
PDQ Security Services, Inc.
1001 Security Blvd Anytown, Ohio 55555
101-555-5000

_____ Date:_____

Authorized by:
_____

Vendor # _____

Date Required _____

Vendor _____ _____ _____
      area code   phone no.   ext.

Ship Via _____

Ship to Attention:

Vendor Name _____

Address _____

_____
department

City _____ State _____ Zip _____

Quantity	X	Stock Number / Description	Per Item	Total Price

IMPORTANT

Our purchase order number must appear on all invoices, packages and correspondence. Acknowledge if unable to deliver by date required. All invoices/statements will be paid 30 days from date of billing.

Accepted by:_____

(Signed):_____

Date _____

8-2 _A typical purchase order._

AGREEMENT TO PROVIDE COMPUTER SERVICES

STATE OF _____

COUNTY OF _____

    This agreement is made and entered into as of the _____ day of _____, 19__ by and between _____ (the Contractor), whose business address is _____ and _____ (the Client), whose business address is_____.

    The Contractor, a computer consultant, offers professional services in support of clients' computer needs, including programming, systems analysis, system design, software analysis, project analysis, project management and facilities management. The Client wishes to retain the Contractor to perform such services, and the Contractor wishes to accept such assignment, on terms and conditions set forth here. Therefore, the parties mutually consent, covenant, represent, warrant and agree as follows:

    Services to be Provided. During the term of this Agreement, the Contractor shall perform the services specified on Exhibit A which is attached made part of this agreeent. The Client agrees to cooperate with _____ in all respects to enable the Contractor to provide the perviccs described. The Client will make available to the Contractor, at the Client's expense, any and all materials and facilities reasonably necessary for the provision of such services, including without limitation, the materials and facilities specified on Exhibit A.

    Personnel. The Contractor agrees to provide such personnel as necessary to provide the services. Such personnel may be employees of the Contractor or independent associates and subcontractors engaged by the Contractor to perform the Services. Any personnel so provided shall at all times be under the supervision and control of the Contractor.

    Term. The period of time during which the Contractor shall perform the services for the Client hereunder is set forth on Exhibit B which is attached and made a part of this contract.

    Fees. In consideration for the services to be performed for the Client by the Contractor, the Client agrees to pay fully and promptly the fees set forth on Exhibit C, attached as a part of this contract. The Client agrees to pay 25% of the total fees set forth on Exhibit C on the date hereof as a retainer or down payment to be applied against the final bill for the services.

8-3 *A simple service agreement, with exhibits.*

Expenses. In addition to the expense of required materials and facilities as provided for in Paragraph 1 and Exhibit A, the Client agrees on demand to pay to or reimburse the Contractor for the expenses set forth on Exhibit D, attached and made part of this contract.

Liability. The Contractor agrees to perform all services in a professional manner and as otherwise set forth in this agreement. The Contractor warrants that custom software written for the Client will perform as specified by the agreement. If the Contractor is unable to cause custom software to perform as agreed, the Client shall be limited in its damages to a refund of the money paid for these services. The Client expressly agrees that neither the Contractor nor his pPersonnel shall be liable to the Client for any loss, liability, damage, cost or expense of the Client (including lost profit or any other direct, indirect or consequential damages) resulting from, or attributable to, performance of the services. Except as provided here, the Contractor neither makes nor intends any express or implied warranties of any type or description including merchantability and/or fitness with respect to the services or any product thereof.

Solicitation of Personnel or Employees. The Contractor agrees that during the term of this agreement and for a period of 180 days after the expiration or termination date of this agreement, it will not, without the prior written consent of the Client solicit, hire, contract with, nor engage the services of, any employee of the Client with whom the Contractor or the Contractor's personnel have worked directly in conjunction with performance of the services. The Client agrees that during the term of this Agreement and for a period of 180 days after the expiration or termination date of this agreement, the Client will not without the prior written consent of the Contractor solicit, hire, contract with, nor engage the services of any personnel of the Contractor.

Non-disclosure by the Contractor. All knowledge and information which the Contractor may acquire from the Client, or from the Client's employees or consultants, or on its premises respecting its inventions, designs, methods, systems, improvements, and other private matters, shall for all time and for all purposes be regarded as strictly confidential and shall not be directly or indirectly disclosed by the Contractor to any person other than to the company without the Client's written permission.

It is further expressly agreed that the Contractor will not intercept any data transmitted through the Client's facilities and that all such data shall be regarded as strictly confidential as described above. However, the Contractor may disclose as part of the Contractor's sales presentations to third parties the following:

The identity of the company and its employee responsible for computer operations; the size and nature of the network--what type of machines are connected with what type of network operating system; the general type of application run on the network, eg., MRP, Word Processing, Spreadsheets.

Non-disclosure by Client. The Client agrees that the method by which the Contractor has networked its computers is a trade secret ofthe Contractor. The Client agrees that the method used shall be for all time and for all purposes regarded as strictly confidential and shall not be directly or indirectly disclosed by company to any person without the prior written permission of the Contractor.

Default. In the event that the Client is in default with respect to any of the provisions of the agreement, the Contractor shall give notice to the Client of its intention to terminate this agreement if such default is not cured to the Contractor's satisfaction within a seven (7) day period. The Contractor shall have the right to terminate this agreement on the first business day following the end of the seven (7) day period. In the event of any such termination, the Contractor shall be entitled to such damages and remedies as are available to it in law or in equity.

Liquidated damages: The parties agree that the damages resulting from a disclosure of confidential information are difficult to establish. They agree that in the event of a breach that portion of this agreement, the damages awarded to the non-disclosing party shall equal three times the amount of the underlying contract(s) for service, together with reasonable attorney's fees. This provision is the exclusive remedy for a breach of the non-disclosure provision, and is in addition to the other remedies that may be available at law or equity for the breach of the other provisions of this agreement.

Parties defined: All references to the Contractor and to the Client include the parties' officers, employees, agents, and independent contractors.

Assignment. A party to this agreement shall not assign or transfer the rights, duties and obligations hereunder unless the other party hereto consents to such assignment in writing prior to any such assignment. Provided, however, that the Contractor may assign, without restriction, its right to payment to a third party as a part of hypothecation of its accounts or otherwise.

Notices. All notices and other communications hereunder must be in writing and shall be deemed to have been given when personally delivered or mailed first class, postage prepaid, addressed to the party to whom such notice is being given at the address set forth in this Agreement. A party may change the address to which such notices shall be given by notifying the other party in accordance with this Paragraph of such change of address.

Severability. Should any provision of this Agreement or part thereof be held under any circumstances in any jurisdiction to be invalid or unenforceable, such invalidity or unenforceability shall not affect the validity or enforceability of any other provision of this Agreement or other part of such provision.

Governing Law. This agreement has been been made and entered into in the State of Maryland, and the construction, validity and enforceability of this Agreement shall be governed by the laws of the State of Maryland.

Entire Agreement. This agreement constitutes the entire agreement between the parties hereto with respect to the subject matter hereof. All prior contemporaneous or other oral or written statements, representations or agreements by or between the parties with respect to the subject matter hereof are merged herein.

Miscellaneous. This agreement shall inure to the benefit of the parties hereto and their respective permitted successors and assigns. This agreement shall not be changed or modified orally but only in writing signed by the parties and stating that it is an amendment to this agreement.

In witness whereof, the Contractor and the Client have caused this agreement to be signed by their respective authorized officers and their respective corporate seals to be hereunto affixed, all as of the day and year first above written.

_____ , Client

By:_____
SEAL

_____ , Contractor

By_____
SEAL

ATTEST by:_____ , Secretary

EXHIBIT A

The services to be performed by _____, Contractor, pursuant to the agreement to which this Exhibit A is attached are as follows:

MATERIALS AND FACILITIES TO BE PROVIDED BY CLIENT

During the term of the agreement to which this Exhibit A is attached, the Client shall provide to the Contractor, at Client's expense, safe and adequate working space and facilities, clerical, typing and technical publication services, machine time, and related services and supplies in addition to the following:

Business hour access to at least one personal computer (IBM AT compatible) with a hard drive, along with the following software: Wordperfect 5.1.

EXHIBIT B

TERM

The services to be provided under this agreement, with this attached Exhibit B, shall commence on _____, 19__ and shall continue until _____, 19__ and, except in the instance of default, shall be extended and continued under the same terms and conditions until written notice of termination of this agreement is given by either party to the other party at least fourteen (14) days prior to the effective date of such notice.

8-3 *Continued.*

EXHIBIT C

FEES

Fees due and payable to the Contractor from the Client under this agreement, with this Exhibit C attached, shall be equal to the gross number of hours worked by the Contractor in providing the services multiplied by a rate of $__.__ per hour. In addition, the Client agrees to pay any and all sales, use, service, or other tax imposed on the Contractor with respect to its rendering the services. Additional fee provisions are as follows:

PAYMENT

At the end of each one-week period during the term of the agreement, beginning with the two-week period immediately following the commencement date of services descri bed here, the Contractor will submit to the Client a statement for services rendered during that period. Such statements shall set forth the number of hours worked during that period by the Contractor, and the total fee due and payable to the Contractor for such services. Payment in full of the fees specified in such statements shall be due and payable within seven days of the date of the statement. If the charges are not paid at the end of the seven days, the Client shall pay on demand to the Contractor a late fee equal to 4% of the unpaid balance of any such statement and, in addition, shall pay to the Contractor interest on the unpaid balance computed on a daily basis from the date of the statement at a rate equal to 1.5% per month, which late fee and interest shall be immediately due and payable.

EXHIBIT D

EXPENSES

Pursuant to the agreement to which this Exhibit D is attached, the Client hereby agrees to pay on demand to or reimburse the Contractor for for the following costs and expenses:

1. Any and all reasonable expenses incurred by the Contractor in training personnel to perform the services:

2. Any and all reasonable travel and living expenses incurred by the Contractor in connection with providing the services, including, but not limited to, air fare, ground transportation, lodging, meals, telephone, parking, and incidentals.

Software licensing agreement   Figure 8-4 presents a portion of a software licensing agreement. The agreement provides a nonexclusive, single-site license in object code form, permits the licensee to transfer the license, offers a 3-year warranty, and will support the product, but wants travel costs.

SOFTWARE LICENSE AGREEMENT

THIS SOFTWARE LICENSE AGREEMENT ("Agreement") is hereby entered into between Peter Hornsback ("Owner") and HRH Communications, Inc. ("Customer") on the following terms and conditions:

1.   License to Software Products.

   (a) Scope of Use. In consideration of Customer's payment of the License Fee with respect to the "Software Products" described on the Product Schedule attached hereto, Customer is granted with respect to each Software Product a paid-up, nonexclusive license ("License") in object code form. Customer may make and use as many copies of the Software Products and associated Documentation as it deems necessary but only for use in support of its (and its affiliates) internal business operations at the single office building (or contiguous set of buildings) at which the Software Products are first installed. This License shall continue for the duration of the Term, as defined in Subsection (c) ("Term, Termination").

   (b) Transfer of License. Customer may transfer its entire License to a Software Product upon advance notice to Owner. Such transfer shall be effective upon the transferee's written agreement to be bound by license terms and conditions applicable to the Software Product hereunder, including Section 6 ("Confidential Information"). After transferring a License, Customer shall return or destroy all copies of the transferred Software Product and shall cease all further use thereof.

8-4   *A main clause in a software licensing agreement. (*Reproduced by permission of Quickform Contracts.*)*

The contract would normally go on to provide clauses covering the term, training, installation, and support, as well as the usual clauses covering payment and late fees, confidentiality, and other standard clauses.

Purchase agreement   Figure 8-5 is an example of a purchase agreement. This agreement assumes that there is no need for confidentiality and non-disclosure clauses, or any clause involving services and their possible effects, much less licensing of any kind. It's of interest to you if you sell some product in addition to your consulting services, and need to contract separately for product sales.

PURCHASE AGREEMENT

STATE OF _____

COUNTY OF _____

Date: _____

_____, Buyer, agrees to purchase from _____, Seller, equipment described in the Exhibit attached, at prices listed therein, which include the State sales tax only. Other taxes and assessments, if any, shall be paid by Buyer, who will pick up the equipemtn at Seller's premises.

Thirty-five percent of the price listed shall be paid on signing this agreement, remainder to be invoiced on date of delivery and paid within 10 days. A late charge of one and one-half percent shall be added to the outstanding charges when account is 30 days past due, and for each month thereafter.

If Buyer refuses to accept any machine or product or Seller must repossess any machine, Buyer shall pay Seller a restocking fee of twenty percent of the purchasse price, plus any damages due as a result of the breach of contract.

Warranty. Equipment is covered by manufacturers' standard warranties. If equipment fails during warranty period, Buyer may deliver the equipment to Seller's place of business for repair. Buyer agrees that Seller shall not be liable for any loss, damage, or expense of Buyer (including any direct, indirect or consequential damages) resulting from, or attributable to the failure of equipment to operate. Seller neither makes nor intends any express or implied warranties, including merchantability and/or fitness with respect to any product thereof.

Title. Title to equipment remains with Seller until full purchase price is paid. Failure to pay the balance of price when due shall give Seller the right, without liability, to repossess the equipment, with or without notice, and to pursue any legal remedy.

Governing Law. This agreement shall be deemed to have been made and entered into in the State of _____ , and the construction, validity and enforceability of this Agreement shall be governed by the laws of the State of

Entire Agreement. This is the entire agreement between the parties with respect to the subject matter hereof. All prior contemporaneous or other oral or written statements, representations or agreements by or between the parties with respect to the subject matter hereof are merged herein.

8-5 *A simple purchase contract for product sales.*

Assignment. A party to this agreement shall not assign or transfer the rights, duties and obligations hereunder unless the other party hereto consents to such assignment in writing prior to any such assignment. Provided, however, that Seller may assign, without restriction, its right to payment to a third party as a part of hypothecation of its accounts or otherwise.

Miscellaneous. This Agreement shall inure to the benefit of the parties hereto and their respective permitted successors and assigns. This agreement shall not be changed or modified orally but only by an instrument in writing signed by the parties which states that it is an amendment to this Agreement.

In witness whereof, Seller and Buyer have caused this agreement to be signed by their respective duly authorized officers and their respective corporate seals to be hereunto affixed, all as of the day and year first above written.

_____ , Seller

BY: _____

Title: _____

ATTEST: _____

BY: _____ , Secretary

_____ , Buyer

By: _____

Title: _____
　　　　(CORPORATE SEAL)

ATTEST: _____

By: _____ , Secretary

Other agreements   There are many other agreements that you might use, directly connected with the services you offer. As a computer consultant, you are likely to enter into agreements for one or more of the following:

- Software maintenance
- Hardware maintenance
- System maintenance
- Escrow (of source code and related materials)

- Software distribution
- Teaming/consortia
- Finder's fees

Some of these—escrow agreements, for example—can be fairly complex, but you can get help. For example, if you elect Data Securities International, Inc. (DSI) as your escrow agent, they will offer you their standard contract form, with whatever options you choose, simplifying your problem substantially.

Combating contract hazards

Even with efforts to keep the contract language as simple and straightforward as possible, the basic agreement in FIG. 8-3 requires four pages—many hundreds of words—and the exhibits require several additional pages, according to how complex the work requirements are. Even four pages can easily influence the client to hesitate. In fact, the agreement itself has little to say about the work to be done, but refers the reader to the exhibit that describes the work requirements. Most of what the basic agreement has to say in its many clauses is defensive and cautionary, written in anticipation of possible problems. Much of it is not necessary because it is redundant, simply citing existing law of the Uniform Commercial Code (UCC) and specific statutes that exist in the state and local legal codes. These statutes are incorporated into every contract, whether the contract specifies it or not. There are cases, however, where the contract can supersede the Code. For example, if the contract makes no statement about assignment, both parties have the right to assign their duties and/or responsibilities arising out of the agreement. The contract in FIG. 8-3, though, stipulates that the parties cannot assign duties or responsibilities.

By not stating whatever the UCC and local statutes already incorporate in the contract, it is possible to reduce most agreements by half or more, thus greatly reducing the formidability of the document, to the betterment of your marketing and sales activity. Retired attorney John Cotton Howell urges that you get a copy of the UCC for your own state, read it through, and keep it at hand for frequent reference, especially with regard to contracts.

Simplifying the language in contracts is a major step forward in making written contracts less formidable without sacrificing the protection a contract gives. One easy way is to write the contract in simple and straightforward English. The *whereases* and *wherefores* are colorful antiquities, but they add nothing to the utility or validity of a contract, and more and more, the legal profession is learning to write briefs and contracts in modern, everyday language. It makes for shorter and easier to understand documents, but most of all, it makes for less hesitancy by clients to closing deals.

9 Common problems & solutions

Every business venture has its share of problems. Consulting is no exception.

A few common business problems

The typical PC consultant is a bright individual with certain well-developed technical and professional skills, but few business skills. In fact, many do not recognize or accept, at first, that consulting is a business and they must be business owners, as well as technical and professional specialists. Many newly established consultants thus make common and understandable mistakes. Some of these are typical of any new, small business, while others are peculiar to consulting. At the same time, there is a certain mythology about consulting, so that it is not always easy to determine which mistakes are based on ignorance and which are based on false beliefs.

Giving the store away

All consultants deal in information and counseling of clients about their special fields. Information and counsel is the principal commodity traded. Because of this, some consultants who write and lecture on the subject of consulting advise caution in providing information on a casual basis. Their theory is that the consultant who answers casual questions and discusses his or her special field without being paid for the conversation is giving away what he or she has to sell. In fact, some suspect that predatory clients deliberately maneuver to pick the brains of the unwary consultant to avoid paying for the help.

Perhaps there is some slight hazard here, but I think it is grossly overestimated. Clients rarely hire a consultant for conversation alone to begin with, so the benefits they would gain from "picking the brains" of anyone would be slight, at best. Clients normally want the consultant to *do* as well as advise. For example, I might advise someone on a marketing problem, but only rarely is that the extent of what I do. I am usually expected to critique existing marketing materials and create new ones or, at least, personally direct and guide their creation.

Even if you do offer some information during a presentation or informal meeting, there is nothing wrong with that. Many companies give samples away to demonstrate value. You might find it worthwhile, even necessary, to do likewise. How else will you demonstrate that you have something of value to offer? In fact, being obviously unwilling to answer innocent questions is likely to have an adverse effect, perhaps to cast doubt on your abilities, and make a prospective client unwilling to consider doing business with you.

Being the "cheapest guy in town"

Many businesses lend themselves to successful operation on the basis of discounts, continual sales, and other bargains. Computer consulting is not such an enterprise. Consulting practices are normally built on confidence in the abilities and integrity of the consultant, and the offer of bargains does not work to create that image. Quite the contrary, it cheapens what you have to offer and gives you the wrong image. Sales and bargains are not usually effective in marketing consulting services.

"Self-employed" or "in business"?

Operating an independent consultancy is self-employment, but it is also a business. Thinking of your consulting practice as a business, rather than as self-employment, offers a certain, subtle advantage in how it shapes your thinking. The "self-employed" concept lures some individuals into seeing themselves simply earning a day's wages every day. As a consultant, however, you should separate yourself into two entities: the business manager and the employee. You must remember, for example, that the salary you draw from your practice is not part of your profit; it is part of the cost of doing business. Profit is what is left, if anything, after recovering all the costs, including that of paying yourself a salary or draw.

Businesses grow on profit, and without it they cannot grow. Thus, your broad goal must always be to pay yourself a reasonable salary—at least as much as you would earn working for someone else, with appropriate benefits—cover all other expenses, including all taxes and overhead, and still have something left after that. What is left—"after taxes," as it is listed on most annual reports—is profit that can be used to finance business growth. It will be used to buy more advanced equipment, fund a newsletter startup, pay for advertising, finance a special promotion, or otherwise pay for growth of any sort that requires expansion of the investment. If business is slow for a time, you can use profit to continue to cover expenses, including your salary.

One problem many home-based consultants have is being completely businesslike in the financial sense. They hesitate to press a slow-paying client to settle the bill, to insist on being reimbursed for reasonable expenses incurred in the course of serving the client's needs, to point out that the client has expanded the original requirement without offering compensating additional payment, or to persuade the client that an expansion of effort is obviously needed. They fear that they will offend the client by pressing in such matters.

I do not recall ever having suffered or being penalized in any way as a result of being completely businesslike with any client, and I have had my share of slow payers and other troublesome clients. Certainly, many clients deliberately "age" their payables in the interests of maximizing their cash flow and minimizing interest charges. However, slow payment is sometimes simply the result of corporate bureaucracy, and I have found clients are often apologetic when I have complained at the slowness of response to my invoices or to other correspondence.

I have also found myself occasionally forced to ask an especially difficult client to please seek help elsewhere to solve his or her future problems. I ask this pleasantly enough, and find the client almost invariably returning to apologize for whatever transgressions offended me, usually with promises to be less offensive in the future! (Many experienced consultants can cite similar hard-to-understand experiences. A few clients apparently choose to be difficult to deal with until they meet with determined resistance.)

Being businesslike applies in many situations, including calling prospects to try to close a sale. It's a mistake to approach prospective clients as a supplicant seeking favors. Prospects sense that attitude, and some try to take advantage of it. You need to know consciously that you have something of value to offer in a trade for dollars, something the other person needs. Thus, you are there merely to explain what it is that you have to offer and negotiate a sale. In short, you are there on equal terms, not as a beggar. It is an important mindset to master. Your own attitude influences others' attitudes toward you.

A poorly understood benefit

The foregoing might sound rather cynical, as if suggesting that you should put on a show to justify high rates. That is not the case at all. The fact is that far too many home-based PC consultants grossly underrate their worth and charge far too little for their services. That's the result of poor marketing—basing one's appeal on price, rather than on quality and benefits. It is, in the end, the benefits of your service that you sell or ought to sell, not your hours and your labor. But do you understand the benefits, all of them? More to the point, do you understand them in the practical terms of the prospect's individual benefit?

There is an obvious direct benefit to you in commanding a high rate for your work: money. But that is not the only benefit. There is a more subtle benefit that rewards both you and your client: Clients are happier—more satisfied—with your work when they have knowingly paid top rates for it and have gotten it delivered with the style that true professionalism dictates. You are far more likely to get complaints from clients to whom you gave special discounts or low rates than from those who paid you what you believed you ought to charge. Those who have nothing else by which to judge will judge by price. High prices mean high quality and great value, and low prices mean low quality and little value.

Of course, a high price alone does not connote high quality. There are other factors, touches that accompany the service and accentuate quality. For example, I take my automobile to the dealer for high-priced service. The floors of the service shop are immaculately clean. The mechanics are in clean uniforms. The upholstery is shielded with a plastic cover. The old parts are placed on the floor of the car in a clean box. A detailed checkoff list of work done is deposited on the seat. Somehow, all of that gives me a comfortable feeling that I am in the best of hands and my car is getting the best attention. It's inherent in the presentation. There is also the impression of solidity and permanence in this dealer's establishment that helps me feel comfortable with him. I am confident that he will be there next month or next year, when I need him again. That comfortable feeling, the confidence in the dealer and his staff, are worth the difference in price to me, as they usually are to most clients.

Creating the perception

Create a confident perception of your abilities by your own presentation of yourself and your service. Perhaps you like to wear jeans, canvas shoes, and a pullover shirt when you are working in your home office, but that is far too casual when with a client. If you want to make the client want to pay you a top rate, wear a well-cut suit, have your shoes shined and your hair trimmed, and if you are a woman, wear small, tasteful jewelry.

Proper dress   How you dress will often be construed to reflect your attitude toward your client. In some recent discussions about this with independent computer consultants, many insisted rather vehemently that computer specialists were entitled to dress casually: sweatshirts, shorts, jeans, and sneakers were implied to be the uniform of the day for computer geniuses. Some people even insisted that a computer consultant who wore a suit and necktie would be considered odd, and not very good at the craft.

I very much doubt that anyone will think you incompetent if you show up on day one at the client's establishment in a suit or dress, with shoes shined and hair trimmed. In fact, it would be awkward if you dressed casually and found everyone in the office in more formal business attire. After that first day, you might want to adapt to whatever appears to be the normal dress in that establishment. However, bear in mind that you are a consultant, not an employee, and you might be expected to adhere to a somewhat different standard than employees do in the matter of proper dress for the office.

Speech   Speak quietly. Make positive statements, but not dogmatic ones. If you have doubts, conceal them and appear confident that you can handle the problem, whatever it is. Be careful about making jokes; it is distressingly easy to give offense, no matter how unintentional. Show respect for the client by listening attentively to what he or she has to say. Refrain from being argumentative when you disagree: Use the "Yes, but" and "You are right, but" approaches to expressing disagreement when you must disagree. (Don't show disagreement at all if it is not necessary to your purposes.)

General knowledge   Keep up technically with what is going on in the computer and consulting fields generally, and your own specialty especially. Know today's equipment and software prices, the state of the art in hardware and software, and what various leading companies are offering. Be able to thus answer clients' casual questions easily, even to the extent of citing articles or reports you have read recently.

When I wanted to buy a new monitor recently, I went to the computer consultant who builds my computers, with complete confidence that he would give me reliable and wise advice. He charges me about a third more than the prices being offered by local discount and mail-order houses, but I pay his prices knowingly and gladly. They are a bargain to me because he gives me such unstinting support and rarely charges me for subsequent service, unless new components are required. I have only once, in the years I have relied on him, been "down" for more than a few hours. That kind of service, support, and dependability are worth money to me, and they are worth money to most clients.

Successful consultants usually make it their business to find time to be active in events related to their profession. They belong to certain associations, participate in meetings and conventions, make public speeches, write for their trade journals, and thus make themselves well-known and well-respected in their fields. These things contribute greatly to your professional image. It's important to find time for some of these activities.

The most important element of your presentation is you, your own bearing and personality. Aside from the externals of physical appearance, there is the more subtle but more important factor of believing in yourself. You must believe that you are worth a top rate. If you do not truly believe it, your client will not believe it. One consultant I knew bought himself an extremely expensive suit. He explained that he wore it only on special occasions, such as meeting or making a presentation to an especially important prospective client. He needed the confidence wearing that marvelous suit gave him. It made him feel 10 feet tall, he said, and even a top corporate officer could not intimidate him then!

Building your self-image

There is nothing magic about coming to believe in yourself and seeing yourself as you want others to see you. It is not a matter of "psyching yourself up" to "believe your own press clippings." It is, instead, an inevitable consequence of doing all the foregoing things—having confidence in your personal appearance, the sense of belonging and contributing from the activities you are involved in, positive feedback from clients and peers. All these things form your self-image without conscious effort on your part. You come inevitably to believe in yourself, to be impressed with yourself and your accomplishments. If you do and are all the things that successful people do and are, you can hardly help but begin to see yourself as a successful person.

Typical financial problems

Every business has financial problems. Many have too little startup capital, and must manage to survive despite that. But even those amply funded for startup and with adequate reserves have financial problems of one sort or another, depending on the nature of the business. Even among PC consultants, financial problems vary with the nature of the consultant's practice and what services he or she sells.

The cash flow problem

Cash flow is a problem of many businesses, especially in times of inflation and high interest rates. Under those conditions, a slowdown in the cash flow is not merely inconvenient, it is costly. It is so costly that many large firms rush their receipts to the bank by special messenger immediately after recording them so that they can gain that same day's interest.

Relatively few businesses are able to make all sales on a strictly cash basis—payment when the service or product is delivered or in advance of delivery. Most businesses must extend credit of some sort, and that is true for the home-based PC consultant, too. Typically, you perform a service and render your bill. The client probably requires a week or more to process your invoice and send you a check. However, most firms today age their payables to minimize problems with their own cash flow, so it is likely that you will wait 30 or even 45 days for payment. Thus, your own cash flow problem can easily become a hardship. It can reach a point where you begin to have trouble paying your bills, even though your practice is profitable on paper, because you are owed more money than you can afford to have owed to you. You simply cannot afford to have so much money "on the street."

If you find yourself with a growing cash flow problem of this description, you must find a way to solve the problem. There are several possible approaches:

- Persuade clients to pay you more promptly.
- Open a line of credit (discount your paper).
- Apply for credit-card merchant status.
- Develop "cash cow" lines to offset the slow-pay problem.
- Combine several of these.

There are a few commonly used methods for trying to persuade clients to pay promptly. One commonly used method is the *prompt payment discount*. You might notice, if you examine the bills you receive from suppliers, a provision that says you may take off two percent of the bill if you pay it in 10 days, one percent if you pay it in 20 days, and *net* (no discount) after that, although payment is due in 30 days.

That, with variations, is a common practice in the business world. Unfortunately, it is only partially effective. All too often, clients take the discount, but still don't pay in less than 30 days, and might take even longer. Thus, the prompt payment discount you offer might boomerang and make an already bad situation worse. In fact, many companies have discontinued offering prompt payment discounts for this reason. You might try it for a time, but be alert for its abuse, and discontinue it if it does not work for you.

Some consultants have gone to the opposite philosophy of charging clients interest or penalties on bills more than 30 days old. That might work for you, but most clients will simply ignore the demand for penalty payments of any kind, confident that you will not risk losing their patronage by pressing that charge.

You might have seen the notices that companies use to remind the client that a bill is overdue. Such notices are usually sent out in a series, starting with a "friendly reminder" and getting more and more stern as time goes on and the bill gets older and older.

After several notices have been sent, most companies take to the telephone to ask directly for payment. It's quite easy to ignore a notice that comes by mail; it isn't nearly as easy to ignore a telephone call. I learned to take to the telephone without mailing out printed notices as soon as a bill was 30 days old and unpaid. I found it far more effective than any other method, whether dealing with an individual, a small company, a large company, or a government agency.

Many times, the problem is simply oversight or bureaucratic inefficiency. In such case, you must persist until you find out exactly what is holding things up. Refuse to accept promises to "get back to you." They are usually meaningless stalls by people who don't want to be bothered tracking down and solving the problem. Insist on finding out what the specific problem is and getting it solved. If necessary, move up the ladder of management until you get to a decision-maker whose command will get people moving. In one case—but only in one case—I had to go to the head of the Department of Commerce about a bill the staff was fumbling over. The department head was annoyed with me, but payment followed.

Discounting your paper

I have been surprised again and again at how many people do not understand this method of getting what clients owe you. The principle is simple enough. You buy an automobile from Joe Smith Pontiac, putting down a few thousand dollars and financing the rest. Shortly after, you get a payment book from a bank or finance company to whom you are to make payments. Or you buy a house from Gordon Home Builders, and you make your mortgage payments to Aggravated Acceptance Corporation.

The organization that sold you the car or house sold your note to a bank or other financing organization. They *discounted your note* by perhaps five or six percent, got their money, and assigned (sold) your note to the other organization, so that you now owe the money to the second organization. The financing organization now handles the account, earning the percentage as their profit for financing the purchase and administering the account.

You can do the same thing, in theory, at least. Once you convince a bank that you and your receivables are solid assets and a good risk, you can make a deal to sell or discount your paper—your receivables—to the bank. It might be *by recourse*, which means that you must indemnify the bank against losses by buying back any receivables that turn into a bad debt, or it might be against a line of credit. In that case, the bank agrees that you can borrow perhaps 85 percent of the face value of your receivables against some line of credit, a maximum sum. You present the bank a certified list of receivables each month, with your request to borrow against your line of credit. Some firms with a high-enough credit rating might not be so constrained, and simply borrow whatever they need against their line of credit.

In some circles, assigning receivables or borrowing against them is known as *factoring*. Not everyone can satisfy the bank that his or her receivables or credit rating merits a line of credit or purchase of receivables, unfortunately. Banks are, of course, quite conservative. But many individuals are in business as factors, handling the accounts the banks reject. Of course, the cost is higher: The factor accepts what is presumably a greater risk than the banks will undertake and so is logically entitled to a greater margin of profit, even if indemnified in the same manner that banks demand. If you cannot sell your receivables to your bank and you need cash to finance your receivables, you might find factoring at least some portion of your receivables a viable alternative. Check the local business publications, where factors often advertise their services.

Merchant status

One way many merchants offer credit to their clients without incurring any great pain and with only minimal risk is via bank credit cards. You might be able to do this, too. While it is theoretically possible to do this with any credit card company, for the purposes of this discussion we will consider only the two popular bank cards, Visa and MasterCard. The use of these two cards is extremely widespread, and can be used in even the smallest establishments. Millions of consumers carry one or both of these cards, and use them as "plastic money" quite regularly. In fact, it is estimated that being in a position to accept payment by credit card can increase your business by from 10 to as much as 50 percent, depending on the type of business you are in.

It is not likely, for example, that large companies retaining you to do computer work for them will offer to pay your bill with a credit card. They are most likely to have agreed to retain you by issuing you a purchase order, and almost surely expect you to submit your bill for payment by company check, if the project is a lengthy one. Credit cards are not normally used for this type of purchase. Thus, the credit card option is useful to you for only certain types of sales and transactions—seminars, product sales, and small service jobs with small companies. It might be helpful, however, if you deal primarily in such services and products.

One problem with accepting credit cards from your customers is that banks have shown a great resistance to granting credit-card *merchant status* to home-based entrepreneurs. There are exceptions, but many home-based consultants report getting credit-card merchant status from banks is an uphill battle. It seems that banks in smaller towns are far more receptive to home-based businesses than banks in major cities, although there have been exceptions here, too. Those who succeed also tend to report that they worked quite energetically at preparing and making a great presentation. That seems to be a major factor in whether the bank is willing to consider granting merchant status to a home-based business.

In any case, there are alternatives if your local banks are unwilling to approve your application for merchant status. Trade associations and local business associations can often help members gain merchant status, and you should investigate that possibility.

There are also organizations that have merchant status and make a business of handling others' credit-card charges for a fee. Unfortunately, some of the fees are on the high side, and some demand up-front investments. Even worse, this practice, while common, is *illegal*. If you are caught, both you and the organization whose merchant status you are using will be blackballed by the credit-card company forever. So, it is far better to try to win your own independent credit-card merchant status.

Progress payments

A small business under contract to the federal government has the right to be paid periodically, as work progresses, and most federal contracting officers agree readily to accepting invoices and making payments every two weeks. Many large corporations follow this same practice on lengthy projects, recognizing the cash-flow difficulty of small businesses. Always inquire of any long-term project whether you can bill every two weeks, as work progresses.

Cash-cow lines   In any business, some activities are more profitable than others or, at least, are cash-up-front activities that produce a steady flow of cash, making it possible to accommodate the slow-paying accounts. These *cash cows* might be logical aspects of your normal practice or spin-offs that turn up serendipitously. On the other hand, it is quite possible to design such activities into your practice deliberately.

Some of the activities discussed in earlier chapters as good PR and added income centers—seminars, training courses, newsletters, and reports—can be important cash cows for your practice, regardless of the field in which you consult. One of the advantages of some of these activities—newsletter subscriptions and seminar registrations, for example—is that you get paid well in advance of delivering the service. That actually puts you ahead of cash-flow curve.

Incidentally, this is an area where credit cards and merchant status can be especially important to you as a client convenience. Many executives use their personal credit cards to travel, attend events, and make purchases that they will eventually charge to their companies on their expense accounts.

Many companies pursue government contracts as cash cows. These contracts might offer only modest profits, but the risk is small, and the cash flow is steady, helping greatly to cover overhead so that other projects are made more profitable.

The IRS & TRA Section 1706   Earlier, I introduced the problem of the IRS' efforts to force computer consultants (and others) working on clients' premises through a broker to be considered employees. Following are the 20 questions of Section 1706, the answers to which supposedly determine whether the individual is entitled to be treated as a contractor (using tax form 1099) or must be an employee (required to file a W2 form).

The logic of the questions is fairly obvious, and there are many consultants who refuse to accept such assignments that would make them W2 employees, rather than 1099 contractors. In any case, knowing these questions can help you avoid being forced into being an employee:

1. Is the person providing services required to comply with instructions about when, where, and how the work is to be done?
2. Is the person provided training to enable him to perform a job in a particular method or manner?
3. Are the services provided integrated into the business' operation?
4. Must the services be rendered personally?
5. Does the business hire, supervise, or pay assistants to help the person performing services under contract?
6. Is the relationship between the individual and the person he performs services for a continuing relationship?
7. Who sets the hours of work?

8. Is the worker required to devote his full time to the person he performs services for?
9. Is the work performed at the place of the business of the potential employer?
10. Who directs the order or sequence in which the work must be done?
11. Are regular oral or written reports required?
12. What is the method of payment—hour, week, commission, or by the job?
13. Are business and/or traveling expenses reimbursed?
14. Who furnishes tools and materials used in providing services?
15. Does the person providing services have a significant investment in facilities used to perform services?
16. Can the person providing services realize both a profit or a loss?
17. Can the person providing service work for a number of firms at the same time?
18. Does the person make his services available to the general public?
19. Is the person providing services subject to dismissal for reasons other than nonperformance of contract specifications?
20. Can the person providing services terminate his relationship without incurring a liability for failure to complete a job?

The IRS much prefers to regard the independent consultant as the temporary employee of the client on the basis provided by Section 1706. If you

- work entirely on the client's premises
- have only one or two clients during the year
- do not have a specific mission or item to deliver
- do whatever work the client specifies each day
- do not maintain a separate business facility
- are required to do the work personally
- are paid by the hour or week
- do not have a specified end-product requirement
- are required to work solely for one client at a time
- do not have an investment in business facilities
- are not incorporated as a business

the IRS will interpret that as *prima facie* evidence that your relationship with the client is that of employee and employer.

Although there are 20 questions which are supposed to resolve the question of whether you are truly an independent consultant and contractor, there are a few principal concerns reflected by those questions. If you can satisfy the IRS of the following, you can make a good case and contest vigorously any efforts on their part to disqualify you as an independent consultant:

- You have many clients (especially concurrently).
- You provide services on your own premises as well as on the client's premises.
- You maintain and operate a proper and adequate service facility (which can be in your own home) that represents a serious investment.

- You have a specified end-product you have agreed to furnish.
- You are properly established as a business entity—properly incorporated or with a registered "dba" (doing business as) trade name.

This problem does not plague every consultant. It is most likely encountered by those whose work normally involves long-term assignments—projects running many months and even years—and those who work on subcontracts to brokers who have signed prime contracts with the client. Typically, you are most likely to encounter such projects and assignments in doing business with government agencies, associations, and other business organizations of substantial size. Theoretically, the standards can be applied to any independent contractor, but in practice, at the time this is written, the IRS appears to be in primary pursuit of consultants working on assignments through brokers—third-party contracting, that is—and not independent consultants making direct deals with clients.

If most of your work involves many clients and short-term assignments and projects that you perform primarily on your own premises, it is not likely that you will run afoul of the IRS in connection with Section 1706. It will seem rather evident that you are indeed an independent consultant, and you can almost surely defend that position and prove that to be the case. Unless Congress changes the law (which might be the case, since there is current corrective legislation being debated), remember the effect on your legal status as an independent consultant when making business decisions. Also, be sure to keep meticulous tax records; software packages such as TaxCut and TurboTax can help.

10 Ethical considerations

Ethics are as much your concern as are the technical aspects of what you do for your clients. There is the moral obligation to do the right thing and refrain from doing the wrong thing, but there is also your own interest—your reputation—at stake. Never underestimate the importance of your reputation; your business survival depends on it.

A consultant's delicate situation

Consulting is more than a special way to practice your profession; it is also a special relationship you must establish and maintain with your clients. It is one thing to sit down at a client's computer and install a word processing program for a client. It is quite another to advise your client on his or her needs or do some special programming for the client.

The difference is quite simple: Installing a program calls for information about the client's peripherals and perhaps personal preferences and work methods. Advising a client regarding special needs or writing new program code is likely to require that you are given access to some of the client's confidential and proprietary information. Or you might come to know some things about a client's business simply because you are on the client's premises, are observant, and the client's employees talk too freely.

Among a lengthy possible list of the kinds of client information that you should consider proprietary and probably confidential are these:

- Marketing data: Who your client does business with, how much business (dollar volume), what kinds of business, names of contacts in those other businesses, and kinds of contracts
- Financial data: The client's total payroll, annual volume, profitability, overhead rate, capital expenditures, and financial position generally
- Suppliers: What the client buys, how much of it, and from whom
- Fringe benefits given to employees
- Typical salary structures
- Personnel policies

Of course, competitors might get some of this information, but they should not get it from you, either directly or indirectly.

Special situations

Unfortunately, the nature of consulting is such that it might sometimes propel you into special situations. A few days after doing a job that makes some of this kind of information available to you, you might be counseling the direct competitor of this client. Be careful to guard your tongue on whatever you have learned of a client's business. Your clients might caution you that certain information you need to do your work is confidential, but even if they do not, you must assume that to be the case. The only safe rule is to assume that anything you know of another client is confidential.

That is only one consideration. Another is that you might work on your client's premises, and as a consultant you might have more privileged access to facilities, as well as information, than employees do. Thus, you must guard your tongue even when talking to the client's staff, remembering that you might have information they do not. You are not morally free to discuss the company's affairs even with the client's own staff. There are many aspects to ethical behavior for consultants. You need, in fact, to adhere to an ethical code of some sort.

An ethical code

The basic element of a proper ethical code is this:

Respect all client confidences, and assume all information given you to be confidential.

This is not, of course, the only element of a proper code of ethics. There is simple honesty. Most employers take it for granted that they will be supplying many basic school supplies for at least some of the children of their employees, no matter how involuntarily or unwillingly they do so. It's almost a natural law. But you are not an employee, and must hold yourself to a stricter code than many employees do.

Even if you observe employees casually helping themselves to the client's property for their personal use, be scrupulously honest with respect to the most insignificant property that belongs to a client. Don't carry the client's pens and pencils away in your pocket, or his paper and notepads in your briefcase. Don't use the client's copying machines for your personal use. Don't make personal calls—at least not toll calls—on the client's telephone. Don't use the client's fax machines for personal transmissions. Don't waste time for which the client is paying you.

In any activity you undertake for a client, the client's perception of fact is what matters, regardless of the actual truth. It's not enough that you know you are honest, trustworthy, and ethical—the client must know it, too.

The client's perception

Thus, it is of utmost importance that you do absolutely nothing that can be misconstrued. If you are overly gregarious in associating with the client's staff, you might arouse suspicion that you are "too friendly" with employees. If you even mention other firms, it might be taken as a signal that you discuss the client with others. If you carry more than necessary in your briefcase when entering or leaving the premises, it might arouse some doubts about your behavior.

Here is a brief list of suggestions to help you project the most favorable image of your discretion and good judgment:

Behavioral guidelines

- Be pleasant and courteous with employees, but maintain a quiet front. Don't have very much to say to anyone, aside from that which is necessary to the work you are doing. Be especially careful to never appear boisterous, even if you are near or with employees who appear to be overcome with good spirits.
- Keep to yourself as much as possible. Don't shun the staff, but don't go out of your way to interact with them.
- Never discuss your work in the company or anything about the company with employees of the company, other than those who are required to work with you.
- Don't gossip, not even about the most harmless items.
- Absolutely minimize your use of the client's telephones, copier, and other facilities.
- Bring your own basic supplies—pencils, pens, notepads—to the job.
- Don't ask employees questions about the company, its executives, or other employees unless they are directly necessary for your work, and then be sure to ask them of the person with whom you are working. Even a casual question asked to make conversation can be construed as an effort to pry or to gain information you do not need and might use adversely.
- Don't make suggestions to employees about finding another job, even if they tell you they are being laid off or are about to start their own independent practice.
- Don't meet with or have conversations with employees outside the office and office hours. This inevitably leaks back to the employer and is taken as a possible cause for suspicion.
- It is best, in preparing brochures, proposals, or other promotional materials, or in making a sales presentation, to refrain from listing other clients or

former clients without their permission. It is especially important that you do not identify or describe the kinds of work you did for such other or former clients, even if you get permission to use their names. Ask how much you may say—whether you may only list them as former clients or may describe in detail what you did for them. Some clients feel, quite understandably, that an explanation of the work you did for them would reveal information about their business that they wish to keep confidential.

Working in private homes

With an estimated 12 million full-time businesses based in the proprietors' homes, sometimes your client's premises will be a private home where he or she has set up an office. In such cases, you are probably dealing with the client directly and exclusively, since most such enterprises involve only the owner or owners. You might meet with your client in his or her living room, feeling very much like an insurance agent rather than a computer consultant!

The atmosphere in this situation might appear more relaxed and informal than it is in a large office with many employees, but don't permit that to lure you into taking liberties, such as being too friendly and informal, no matter how jovial and easy-going the client appears to be. It is still a business environment. The client who owns a small, home-based enterprise is entitled to as much respect and courtesy as the president of a large corporation, and the same standards of ethics apply.

A sticky situation

On some occasion you might be working for a client who knows you have worked with one or more of his or her competitors, and expects you to make what you know of competitors available to him or her. This can put you into an especially tricky and difficult predicament: You want to do the best you can for each client, but you know that it is wrong to leak information from one to the other.

What you do when a client pressures you to leak confidential information is up to you, but think about it first. Be aware that the client to whom you leak information now knows that you can be "gotten" and will react to you with the knowledge that you might leak what you know of him or her to another competitor. It is thus very much in your interest—mandatory, in my opinion—that you decline to supply the information, even if it costs you the assignment. It probably will not, and the client might even have been testing you. (I have been so tested by clients myself on more than one occasion, and at least one told me that I would have been "out the door" quite promptly, had I succumbed to his pleas.)

Contracting: An ethical dilemma

Many consultants pursue large contracts that call for formal bids or even proposals. If you do this, but also accept many small on-site projects, you might find yourself in another kind of ethical dilemma: In pursuing a large contract requiring a bid, proposal, or formal presentation, you might be competing against a client or former client about whom you have confidential information. Do you use this information to win the competition?

Many consultants might answer this question immediately: "Certainly." There is the practical question of whether it is in your best interests to do so, of course, but that is not the question here. Here, the question is whether it is ethical and moral to use information gained in confidence to compete against the former client.

The proper answer, in my opinion, must be "It depends." You can hardly help but use what you know to write the best bid, proposal, or presentation possible in terms of presenting your own position. Actually presenting specific information about a former client in doing so, however, is a wrong, morally and ethically. ("Knocking" competitors, in general, is poor policy, even when they are total strangers and you are criticizing them in an indirect manner. Many clients are outraged at such behavior.)

You might do business occasionally or regularly by winning subcontracts, whether from a broker who specializes in finding subcontractors to work on clients' sites, or from a technical services firm that undertakes entire projects and needs some help. (Such firms often subcontract portions of the project.) Or you might hire out to a "job shop"—a supplier of professional and technical temporaries—and thus be assigned to work on the premises of the supplier. This can lead to other special situations.

Subcontracting & job shopping

In these cases, the prime contractor is your client, and what has been said earlier applies equally here. The job shop that hires you, for example, is technically and legally your employer, but it is a good idea to regard the shop as your client, especially since your tenure with the shop is likely to be relatively short, but you might want to be employed by them again at some time. When you work for another contractor or a job shop, there are a few special concerns:

- Working on the premises of someone else's client means that you represent that company. What you do reflects on them, as well as on you. At the same time, you must handle yourself as if this were your own direct client, with the same commitment to absolutely ethical behavior.
- This client might ask you to either contract directly with him or her, rather than supporting him or her via a third party, or even to become an employee. (This is a fairly common event, one that I encountered occasionally in the years that I worked as a professional/technical temporary.) That poses special ethical concerns. You might have signed a non-compete agreement (see chapter 8) in accepting the work. That is a fairly common practice and not unreasonable, if the non-compete period is not more than one year. Even if you have not signed such an agreement, you have a moral obligation to do the right thing. At least, you are morally obligated to discuss the offer with your client or employer before taking any action. Job shops sometimes ask clients to agree to pay a placement fee if they wish to hire a temporary, for example, and that would make clear

what you could do ethically, but you might not know unless you ask whether special arrangements or understandings are in place.

- Brokers and job shops are run by smart, tough business people, engaged in highly competitive businesses. They negotiate well and bargain relentlessly. Most of us pay for our lack of experience the first time we do business with them. Some consultants therefore rationalize that they have no ethical obligations when doing business with these kinds of firms. They rationalize also that non-compete agreements are immoral, difficult to enforce, and possibly even illegal. That might be true, but whether it justifies sharp or unscrupulous behavior on your own part is up to you to decide.

My own view is that you owe ethical and honorable behavior to yourself, if not to a client or employer. It is as important to your relationships and probability of repeat business as is honesty in your billing and guaranteeing your work.

Profile: Fees, contracts, & ethics

Paul Cote has operated F1 Consulting Services from his home in a small town north of Toronto for 4½ years. Cote began his computer career writing code, but quickly switched to sales when he realized he liked being with people more than programming. He worked in computer sales for eight years before leaving to become a consultant. He explains, "In sales, I couldn't recommend another product even if I knew it was better. As a consultant, I can provide small businesses unbiased DP support."

Cote's home office is quite large and well-equipped. He recalls, "I started out in a spare room. Then, when we moved, I took over the living room, plus a second office [for his part-time clerical help]. It's about 700 square feet, total." Cote has a business telephone system with four lines, a fax machine, photocopier, and several PCs. Despite the fact that he is better equipped than many office buildings, he still senses a stigma associated with home-based computer consultants, that they are somehow amateur and so should charge less than a large consulting company. In fact, Cote does charge considerably less than his major competitor, a Big 10 firm, but he makes clear to his clients that the lower price is a result of his more efficient operation and lower overhead, not a lack of expertise.

Fee structure

Cote structures his fees the way his major clients—lawyers, accountants, and other professionals—do. His 20 regular clients pay him a retainer based on 15 hours per month at $45 per hour. This minimizes his cash flow problems, and gives clients the security of knowing they can call whenever they have questions or problems. Over the course of a year, Cote says the hours usually work out, "If they don't use up the hours one month, it evens out the next. If they go over, I charge at the $45 rate." He reports no resistance to this fee structure; his clients are used to a retainer because that is how many of them charge their own clients. Occasional or new clients are billed at $65 per hour, with the first visit free. Again, this is similar to the way other professionals bill.

Cote is quite sensitive to overcharging; in fact, he acknowledges a tendency to undercharge. He believes strict attention to clients' budgets is especially important in the relatively small, rural community he serves. As he explains, "The mentality is different in a small community. It might take a client six to nine months to decide to spend $15,000. It's not like in a big city where businesses make $40,000 decisions over lunch. Also, every vendor wants to be a consultant, too, so it's very competitive."

Because of this, Cote has occasionally discounted his rate for the first job with a new client, but finds he doesn't need to do it often anymore. So far, he hasn't lost any clients changing to his regular rates on subsequent jobs, although he admits, "Nobody wants to pay the price on the ticket."

Using contracts

Cote has tried a number of approaches to client contracts. When he first started F1 Consulting Services, he met with a lawyer to have a formal, standard contract drawn up. However, the resulting contract was eight pages long—much too long and complicated for his purposes.

Next, he tried a $150 software program that generates standard computer-industry contracts. He uses this for a few clients, but says, "For most people, even walking in with a two-page contract would scare them away."

Now, based on the size of the project and his relationship with the client, he most often uses a simple letter of agreement or verbal agreement. This relatively casual relationship has served Cote quite well. He reports, "I only got burned once, in the first year I was in business—by a lawyer!"

A code of ethics

Cote believes quite strongly in the need for an ethical code among computer consultants, "There are a lot of unethical people in this business. We're the only profession with no formal, enforced code of ethics." He promotes regulation of computer consultants and compliance to an ethical code as a board member of the Independent Computer Consultants Association (ICCA).

Cote's personal code is made up of the following:
- Do not take any type of job that you cannot do. For example, if a client needs custom database programming or training, Cote subcontracts or refers the job to another consultant who specializes in those areas.
- Be up front always, with all clients. Cote believes computer consultants should be completely independent, with absolutely no relationships with vendors. That way, there is no danger of recommending a solution simply because you owe the vendor a favor. Cote doesn't even make large

purchases for his own business from local vendors to avoid the impression of bias.

- Confidentiality "goes without saying." Cote sees a lot of personal information, especially since many of his clients are doctors, lawyers, and accountants. He scrupulously guards this information, knowing that "you can do 150 things right, and nobody says anything, but if you do one thing wrong, everyone hears. You have to be trusted to succeed in this business."

Cote urges new PC consultants to join an organization such as ICCA. He believes the chance to talk to people in the business regarding such issues as contracts and ethics is critical to the growth of the individual consultant and the industry as a whole.

Resource guide

Henry Ford once remarked, from the witness stand in a courtroom, that it was unnecessary for him to learn anything that he could easily find out about if he needed the information. That has the seeds of wisdom in it for all of us, especially in this age of information. It is, in fact, the idea behind furnishing a reference section, such as this.

I have tried here to pass on as much of what I have learned about consulting as I could fit into these pages. This appendix exists to direct you to additional resources of various kinds to help you learn more about those topics that interest you especially and that support your consulting practice.

Useful periodicals

Corporate Meetings & Incentives
Harcourt Brace Jovanovich Publications
1 East First Street
Duluth, MN 55802
A trade paper for those planning or hosting meetings

Direct Response Specialist
P.O. Box 1075
Tarpon Springs, Florida 34286-1075
A monthly newsletter of direct-marketing ideas and guidance by direct-mail consultant Galen Stilson

DM News
19 West 21st Street
New York, NY 10010
A weekly tabloid on direct marketing

Entrepreneur
Entrepreneur Group, Inc.
2392 Morse Avenue
Irvine, California
A thick periodical, full of business ideas

Home Office Computing
Scholastic, Inc.
730 Broadway
New York, NY 10003
The most directly relevant magazine listed here, found on newsstands

Income Opportunities
Davis Publications, Inc.
380 Lexington Avenue
New York, NY 10017
A magazine for "opportunity seekers," with many articles and advertisements of interest to those seeking to build a home business; found on newsstands

The Khera Business Report
Khera Communications, Inc.
P.O. Box 8043
Gaithersburg, MD 20898-8043
This four-page, monthly newsletter is aimed specifically at independent PC consultants. The annual rates-survey issue can be particularly informative.

Meeting News
Gralla Publications
1515 Broadway
New York, NY 10036
A trade paper of hotels and others with an interest in meetings and other gatherings

Meetings & Conventions
Ziff-Davis
One Park Avenue
New York, NY 10016
Still another trade publication for those with an interest in meetings

Sharing Ideas!
P.O. Box 1120
Glendora, CA 91740
A bimonthly periodical published by Dottie Walters that has become almost the bible of the public-speaking industry, but is also of interest to writers and consultants

Target Marketing
401 North Broad Street
Philadelphia, PA 19108
A monthly slick paper trade magazine for direct marketers

Organizations in public speaking

Many successful consultants are also speakers, lecture agents, publishers, and trainers of speakers. In fact, the skills of speaking, writing, and consulting complement each other surprisingly well. There are a number of speakers associations. Here are several you should know about:

National Speakers Association (NSA)
5201 North 7th Street, Suite 200
Phoenix, AZ 85014

International Platform Association (IPA)
2564 Berkshire Road
Cleveland Heights, OH 44106

Toastmasters International, Inc.
P.O. Box 10400
Santa Ana, CA 92711

There is a great abundance of mailing list brokers, firms from whom you can rent (and in some cases buy) mailing lists. You can find them listed in the yellow pages, as well as in many other media. Here are just a few of them, many of them branch offices of mailing list firms:

Mailing list brokers

Allmedia, Inc.
4965 Preston Park Boulevard
Plano, TX 75093

Jami Marketing Services
2 Bluehill Plaza
Pearl River, NY 10965

American List Counsel, Inc.
88 Orchard Road
Princeton, NJ 08543

Listworks
One Campus Drive
Pleasantville, NY 10570

AZ Marketing Services, Inc.
31 River Road
Cos Cob, CT 06807

Qualified Lists Corporation
135 Bedford Road
Armonk, NY 10504

The Coolidge Corporation
25 West 43rd Street
New York, NY 10036

Woodruff-Stevens & Associates
345 Park Avenue South
New York, NY 10010

Dependable Lists, Inc.
950 South 25th Avenue
Bellwood, IL 60104

Worldata
5200 Town Center Circle
Boca Raton, FL 33486

Direct Media
200 Pemberwick Road
Greenwich, CT 06830

Many of those who belong to speakers' associations (listed earlier) are consultants. But there are also a number of consultants' associations, over 30, in fact. Many of them are highly specialized, and would be of little interest to you as a computer consultant. Following are a few that may be of interest to you:

Consultant associations

American Association of Professional Consultants
9140 Ward Parkway
Kansas City, MO 64114

American Consultants League
1290 Palm Avenue
Sarasota, FL 34236

Association of Management Consultants
500 North Michigan Boulevard
Chicago, IL 60611

Independent Computer Consultants Association
933 Gardenview Office Parkway
St. Louis, MO 63141

Society of Professional Business Consultants
221 North LaSalle Street
Chicago, IL 60601

Society of Professional Management Consultants
16 West 56th Street
New York, NY 10019

Home-based business resources
American Home Business Association
60 Arch Street
Greenwich, CT 06830
203-661-0105 and 800-433-6361

Center for Home-Based Businesses
Truman College
1145 West Wilson
Chicago, IL 60640
312-989-612

National Association for the Self-Employed
2316 Gravel Road
Ft. Worth, TX 76118

National Association of Home-Based Businesses
P.O. Box 30220
Baltimore, MD 21270

Service Corps of Retired Executives (SCORE)
1825 Connecticut Avenue, NW
Washington, DC 20009
202-653-6279
SBA-sponsored volunteer consultants

Small Business Administration,
Office 1441
L Street, NW
Washington, DC 20416
Headquarters of about 80 district offices, distributed across major cities. SBA now has a BBS, SBA ONLINE (1-800-859-4636), and invites everyone to call and take advantage of SBA services.

Consultant labor contractors

Many computer consultants accept assignments through organizations that provide technical and professional temporaries, acting as brokers or job shops (see chapter 8). There are hundreds of such firms, many of whom advertise widely in the help-wanted columns. The following is only a brief starter list of such brokers that have many offices in various locations.

Consultants and Designers
300 West 31st Street
New York, NY 10001

Tad Technical Corporation
639 Massachusetts Avenue
Cambridge, MA 02139

Day & Zimmerman, Inc.
1818 Market Street
Philadelphia, PA 19103

Volt Information Sciences, Inc.
101 Park Avenue
New York, NY 10017

For retirees & older workers

The National Association of Temporary Services (NATS) furnishes a list of offices that deal exclusively in placing senior citizens in temporary positions. Some of them deal in all kinds of workers, while others deal only in one or two specific skills. The following offices place technical and professional people. The companies to which they belong are all national companies, which means that each has at least 10 offices operating in at least 10 different states. A contact is identified for each.

Although the following specialize in placing older workers, that does not mean that other offices will not also place older workers. Note that each of these offices is only one of many operated by company. Don't hesitate to get in touch with any of the other offices of the company. You are likely to find other offices listed in your own yellow pages directory, but if none of the following are in a location that is convenient for you, don't hesitate to call any of these and ask for directions to other offices of their company closer to you. It is a perfectly reasonable and sensible thing to do.

Accounting/Robert Half Inc.
Max Messmer
100 Bush Street, Suite 1700
San Francisco, CA 94104
415-788-7030
201 offices

Adia Personnel Services
Walter Macauley
64 Willow Place
P.O. Box 2768
Menlo Park, CA 94022
415-324-0696
750 offices

Career Horizons, Inc.
Joel B. Miller
695 East Main Street
Financial Centre
Stamford, CT 06901
203-975-8001
166 offices

Dunhill Temporary Systems
Howard Scott
P.O. Box 137
Paoli, PA 19301-0237
516-364-8800
51 offices

Express Temporary Services
Bob Funk
6300 Northwest Expressway
Oklahoma City, OK 73132
405-840-5000
130 offices

Kelly Services, Inc.
Terance E. Adderley
999 West Big Beaver Road
Troy, MI 48084
313-362-4444
850 offices

Manpower, Inc.
Mitchell Fromstein
5301 North Ironwood Road
P.O. Box 2053
Milwaukee, WI 53201
820 offices

Office Specialists
Robert M. Whalen
Corporate Place
128 Audubon Road, Building 1, #3
Wakefield, MA 01880
617-246-4900
50 offices

The Olsten Corporation
Frank Liguori
One Merrick Avenue
Westbury, NY 11590
516-832-8200
500 offices

Remedy Temporary Services
Robert McDonough
32122 Camino Capistrano
San Juan Capistrano, CA 92675
714-661-1211
40 offices

Salem Services, Inc.
J. Marshall Seelander
1333 Butterfield Road
Downers Grove, IL 60515
708-515-0500
36 offices

Snelling & Snelling, Inc.
Brian Dailey
4000 South Tamiami Trail
Sarasota, FL 33581
813-922-9616
87 offices

Talent Tree, Inc.
Mike Willis
9703 Richmond Avenue
Houston, TX 77042
713-974-6509
104 offfices

Uniforce Temporary Services
Rosemary Maniscalco
1335 Jericho Turnpike
New Hyde Park, NY 11040
516-437-3300
81 offices

Volt Temporary Services
Mary Smith
2401 N. Glassell Street
P.O. Box 13500
Orange, CA 92665
714-921-8800
83 offices

The following is a brief sampling of a few better-known online utilities and public databases. They are available on a subscription basis, usually with a "connect time" charge and a monthly minimum. The main difference between a database and a utility is that the public database is strictly an information source and usually used only by those who need the information for business and professional purposes, while an online utility also offers services for entertainment and amusement.

Online utilities & public databases

CompuServe Information Service, Inc.
5000 Arlington Centre Boulevard
Columbus, OH 43220
800-848-8900
617-457-8600

GEnie
GE Information Services
401 North Washington Street
Rockville, MD 20850
800-638-9636
301-340-4000

Prodigy Services Company
445 Hamilton Avenue
White Plains, NY 10601
914-993-8848

Minitel USA
1700 Broadway
New York, NY 10019
212-307-5005

Online utilities

Dialog Information Services, Inc.
3460 Hillview Avenue
Palo Alto, CA 94304
800-334-2564
415-858-3792

BRS Information Technologies
1200 Route 7
Latham, NY 12110
800-227-5277
518-783-7251

Dow Jones News Retrieval
P.O. Box 300
Princeton, NJ 08543-0300
800-522-3567
609-452-1511

NewsNet, Inc.
945 Haverford Road
Bryn Mawr, PA 19010
800-345-1301
215-527-8030

Mead Data Central
9393 Springboro Pike
P.O. Box 933
Dayton, OH 45401
800-227-4908

Public databases

Government BBSs

Many bulletin board systems (BBSs) are operated in federal government offices. Some are official organs of the agencies, while others are quasi-official in that an employee operates them under the sponsorship of the agency. One of the most important of these for a computer consultant is the General Services Administration, which has jurisdiction over computer standards-setting and other matters relating to computer procurement by government agencies. This bulletin board carries important information about requirements, procurements, and major contractors, so it can be an important source of business leads for you.

General Services Administration BBS
202-501-2014
A message on this BBS provides a list of telephone numbers for each of the 10 GSA regional contacts for ADP Technical Service Requirements contracts as follows:

Region 1	617 835-5753
Region 2	215 597-5104
Region 3	215 597-5104
Region 4	205 895-5091
Region 5	312 886-3824
Region 6	816 926-5610
Region 7	817 334-1684
Region 8	303 236-7319
Region 9	415 974-7557
Region 10	206 442-2418

Another highly important BBS is that run by the Small Business Administration. The toll-free number for SBA ONLINE at 2400 baud is given earlier in this appendix, but there are two other numbers for SBA ONLINE:

202 205-7265
800 697-4636 *access at 9600 baud*

Some of the many other BBS in government offices are listed here:

U.S. Navy
Navy ADA Language System: 703-614-0215

Department of Agriculture Library: 800-345-5785 or 301-504-6510
Nutrition: 301-436-5078

Library of Congress
ALIX II: 202-707-4888

Department of Commerce
Census Bureau: 301-763-4574
Geological Survey: 703-648-4168

Department of Education: 202-219-2011 or 202-219-2012
Department of Interior: 703-787-1181

State Department
U.S.A.I.D./Permanet BBS: 703-715-9806 (2400 baud) or 703-715-9851 (9600 baud)

National Science Foundation
SRS (Science and Research Studies): 202-634-1764

Government Printing Office
Federal Bulletin Board: 202-512-1387

The Institute for Certification of Computer Professionals (ICCP) offers certification programs. Write or call for details:

Certification

2200 East Devon Avenue, Suite 268
Des Plaines, IL 60018
708-299-4227 (telephone)
708-299-4280 (fax)

Bibliography

Arth, Marvin and Ashmore, Helen, 1980. *The Newsletter Editor's Desk Book*. Shawnee Mission: Parkway Press.

Bly, Robert W., 1985. *Create the Perfect Sales Piece*. New York: John Wiley.

Bove, Tony, Cheryl Rhodes, and Wes Thomas, 1986. *The Art of Desktop Publishing*. New York: Bantam.

Broudy, Eve, 1989. *Professional Temping*. New York: Collier Books.

Burgett, Gordon, and Mike Frank, 1985. *Speaking for Money*. Carpinteria: Communication Unlimited.

Cohen, William A., 1983. *The Entrepreneur & Small Business Problem Solver*. New York: John Wiley.

Edwards, Paul and Sarah, 1985. *Working from Home*. Los Angeles: Jeremy P. Tarcher.

Elliott, Susan, 1985. *Ideas That Work: Ten of Today's Most Exciting and Profitable Self-Employment Opportunities*. Boulder: Live Oak Publications.

Glenn, Peggy, 1983. *Word Processing Profits at Home*. Huntington Beach: Aames-Allen Publishing.

Glossbrenner, Alfred, 1984. *How to Get Free Software*. New York: St. Martin's Press.

_____, 1990. *The Complete Handbook of Personal Computer Communications, 3rd ed.*, New York: St. Martin's Press.

Goldstein, Arnold S., and Robert L. Davidson, III, 1992. *Starting Your Subchapter "S" Corporation*. New York: John Wiley.

Herman, Jeff, 1993. *Insider's Guide to Book Editors, Publishers, and Literary Agents*. Rocklin, CA: Prima.

Hoge, Cecil, Sr., 1976. *Mail Order Moonlighting*. Berkeley: Ten Speed Press.

Holtz, Herman, 1986. *The Consultant's Guide to Proposal Writing, 2nd ed.* New York: John Wiley.

_____, 1988. *The Consultant's Guide to Winning Clients*. New York: John Wiley.

_____, 1992. *Databased Marketing*. New York: John Wiley.

_____, 1986. *The Direct Marketer's Work Book*. New York: John Wiley.

_____, 1992. *How to Start and Run a Writing & Editing Business*. New York: John Wiley.

_____, 1988. *How to Succeed as an Independent Consultant, 2nd ed.* New York: John Wiley.

_____, 1983. *Secrets of Practical Marketing for Small Business.* Englewood Cliffs: Prentice-Hall.

_____, 1985. *Speaking for Profit.* New York: John Wiley.

Hyypia, Erik and the editors of Income Opportunities, 1992. *Crafting the Successful Business Plan.* Englewood Cliffs: Prentice-Hall.

Jacobi, Peter P., 1991. *The Magazine Article.* Cincinnati: Writer's Digest Books.

Kamoroff, Bernard, 1985. *Small Time Operator.* Laytonville: Bell Springs.

Khera, Raj, 1992. *Current computer consulting rates. The Khera Business Report*, Fall 1992.

_____, 1993. *Pricing your professional services. The Khera Business Report*, April 1993.

Kissling, Mark, editor, 1991. *1992 Writer's Market.* Cincinnati: Writer's Digest Books.

Kravitt, Gregory I., 1993. *Creating a Winning Business Plan.* New York: Probus.

Lewis, Herschell Gordon, 1984. *Direct Mail Copy That Sells.* Englewood Cliffs: Prentice-Hall.

Mancuso, Joseph R., 1985. *How to Write a Winning Business Plan.* Englewood Cliffs: Prentice-Hall.

McKeever, Mike, 1992. *How to Write a Business Plan.* New York: Nolo Press.

Newman, Edwin, 1980. *On Language.* New York: Warner Books.

Ries, Al and Jack Trout, 1993. *The 22 Immutable Laws of Marketing.* New York: Harper Business.

Schectman, Gilbert, 1992. *Getting Down to Cases: Scenarios for Report Writing.* Englewood Cliffs: Prentice Hall.

Siegel, Eric S., Brian R. Ford, and Jay M. Bornstein, 1993. *The Ernst & Young Business Plan Guide, 2nd ed.* New York: John Wiley.

Touchie, Rodger, 1989. *Preparing a Successful Business Plan: A Practical Guide for Small Business.* Vancouver: Self-Counsel Press.

Varner, Iris I., 1991. *Contemporary Business Report Writing, 2nd ed.* Chicago: Dryden Press.

Wilder, Claudyne, 1990. *The Presentations Kit.* New York: John Wiley.

Wohlmuth, Ed, 1990. *Overnight Guide to Public Speaking.* Philadelphia: Running Press.

Index

***Boldface** page numbers refer to art

*****Boldface** page numbers refer to art

*****Boldface** page numbers refer to art

training services, 49-50, 109
types of PC users, 44-47
  business-use users, 45
  common factors of all PC owners, 46-47
  home-based-business users, 45-46
  network PC users, 46
  organizations using PCs, 46
  personal-use users, 44-45
  single- vs. multiple-PC owners, 46

U

Uniform Commercial Code, contracts, 121, 123, 136
user groups, xi, 42

V

variances, zoning laws, 16

W

Wilson, Steve, 16
"worry items" in proposals, 81-82
writing skills, 91-104
  advantages of written over spoken presentations, 93
  audiotape production, 100, 110-111
  book writing, 99-100, 101
  consulting via writing, 109
  copyrighting materials, 100
  importance of writing/speaking, 91-92
  learning to write, 92-93
  licensing others to use copyrighted material, 100
  Literary Marketplace (LMP), 99
  newsletters, 94-98, 101, 111, **112**
  periodical/magazine articles, 98-99, 101, **103**
  proposals, 111, 113
  seminars, 105-109, 110
  technical writing, 94-95
  tips for successful writing, 94
  training services for clients, 109
  writing for publication 58-59, 98-100

Z

zoning laws, 15-16

"People are thirsty for specific how-to information that can enable them to earn a living at home," say Paul and Sarah Edwards, authors of *Working from Home* and *Best Home-Based Businesses for the Nineties*.

The Windcrest/McGraw-Hill Entrepreneurial PC series is designed to fill the until-now unmet need for step-by-step guidance for people wanting to make the work-home transition. The Edwards' track the trends that yield opportunities for successful home-based businesses and then find authors to provide the nitty-gritty business-specific information that can spare the home-based entrepreneur months of frustration and costly mistakes.

Paul and Sarah have been working from their home since 1974. It didn't take them long to realize they were participating in what would become a major social and economic trend—the home-based business. That spurred them to want to help others make the transition from office to home and to professionalize the image of home-based business.

Paul and Sarah are contributing editors to *Home Office Computing* magazine and write the monthly column, "Ask Paul and Sarah." They founded and manage the *Working From Home Forum* on CompuServe, an electronic network with more than 30,000 people around the world who work from home. Paul and Sarah also cohost the hour-long national weekly radio program "Home Office" on the Business Radio Network.

About the author

Herman Holtz is the author of 49 business and professional how-to books, including the bestseller, *How to Succeed as an Independent Consultant*, which has sold over 100,000 copies. Holtz has done consulting work for IBM, RCA, General Electric, Chrysler Corporation, and many other Fortune 500 companies. In addition, he is a nationally known authority on government consulting and on building a successful independent consulting practice.